I ♥ MY SLOW COOKER

I  MY SLOW COOKER

MORE THAN 100 OF THE BEST EVER RECIPES

BEVERLY LeBLANC

NOURISH

EAT WELL, LIVE WELL

I Love My Slow Cooker
Beverly LeBlanc

First published in the USA and Canada in 2012 by
Nourish, an imprint of
of Watkins Publishing Limited
PO Box 883, Oxford, OX1 9PL

A member of Osprey Group
enquiries@nourishbooks.com

Osprey Publishing
PO Box 3985
New York, NY 10185-3985
Tel: (001) 212 753 4402
Email: info@ospreypublishing.com

Managing Editor: Grace Cheetham
Editors: Krissy Mallett and Jo Murray
Americanizer: Beverly LeBlanc
Managing Designer: Manisha Patel
Design and photography art direction: Paul Reid at cobalt id
Production: Uzma Taj
Commissioned photography: William Lingwood
Food Stylist: Lucy Mckelvie
Prop Stylist: Liz Hippisley

ISBN: 978-1-84899-267-2

10 9 8 7 6 5 4 3 2 1
Typeset in Adobe Garamond Pro and Calibri
Color reproduction by Colourscan
Printed in China

To PMOB

Publisher's note: While every care has been taken in compiling the recipes for this book, Watkins Publishing Limited, or any other persons who have been involved in working on this publication, cannot accept responsibility for any errors or omissions, inadvertent or not, that may be found in the recipes or text, nor for any problems that may arise as a result of preparing one of these recipes. If you are pregnant or breastfeeding or have any special dietary requirements or medical conditions, it is advisable to consult a medical professional before following any of the recipes contained in this book.

Vegetarian Recipes
Vegetarian recipes in this book contain no meat, poultry, game, fish or shellfish. They can include eggs or cheese. Cheese, especially those made using traditional methods, might contain calf rennet, so check labels first. Look for "suitable for vegetarians," or "contains vegetarian rennet" on the label.

Notes on the recipes
Unless otherwise stated:
All recipes serve 4
All recipes have been tested in a 4-quart oval slow cooker
Use large eggs and medium fruit and vegetables
Use fresh ingredients, including chilies, unless otherwise specified
All-purpose and self-rising flour is to be measured by spooning into the cup measure and leveling
1 tsp. = 5ml 1 tbsp. = 15ml 1 cup = 240ml

Author's Acknowledgments
Thank you to all the team at Nourish—especially Grace Cheetham, Krissy Mallett and Jo Murray—for the care and attention put into this book. As always, you were a pleasure to work with.
  Big thank yous and much appreciation also go to my recipe testers—Philip Back, Philip Clarke, Christa Langan and Veronica Martell—to Carl Cullingford, Jean Herbert, Maggi Gordon, Rita Kandela and Janet Podolak (and their families and friends) for their helpful suggestions and ideas, and to the butchers at Macken Brothers, Chiswick, London.

Watkins Publishing is supporting the Woodland Trust, the UK's leading woodland conservation charity, by funding tree-planting initiatives and woodland maintenance.

nourishbooks.com

CONTENTS

INTRODUCTION

I only developed my appreciation of the benefits of slow-cooker cooking relatively late in my culinary career. And, like any new convert, I want to share my enthusiasm.

Slow cookers are simple electrical appliances which, as the name implies, slowly cook food with indirect low-heat transfer in a moist environment. The temperature inside the pot builds up slowly and then remains constant, so slow cookers are especially good at cooking one-pot favorites like casseroles, curries, soups, stews and tagines. They are also versatile enough to cook pot roasts, poultry, roasts, rice and many desserts.

Slow cookers were first developed in the United States in the 1960s, where they were used to cook beans on an industrial scale. In the 1970s, they were embraced by the domestic market as more women entered the workforce. Later, as microwaves and prepared meals became commonplace, slow cookers fell from favor and developed a bad reputation for producing flavorless, mushy food.

Today, however, slow cookers are enjoying a revival. They are back in pride of place on kitchen counters, as people with busy and unpredictable lifestyles appreciate how versatile the slow cooker is at producing wholesome meals. If you only remember the insipid slow-cooker dishes of the past you are in for a treat as you work your way through this collection of recipes inspired by cuisines from around the world.

The outstanding feature that makes slow cookers such an important part of contemporary kitchens, however, is that once you push the button to start the cooking process, most recipes require no more attention until just before serving. Because there isn't any danger of ingredients catching or burning on the bottom, you don't have to constantly stir, or monitor the progress. It's a great comfort to leave the house confident a delicious, satisfying evening meal will be waiting for you when you return. If you invest in a modern model with a programmable timer, you don't even have to worry about dinner overcooking and spoiling if you are delayed, as the slow cooker automatically switches itself to a WARM setting (see page 9).

Slow cookers can also help stretch your budget in two ways. The moist, slow cooking process is excellent for tenderizing inexpensive cuts of meat, an important consideration for anyone wanting to cut their food bills. The cookers are also more economical to run than other conventional cooking methods, such as casseroling on the stovetop or in the oven. Almost all manufacturers make the claim that leaving a slow cooker to cook all day is no more expensive than leaving a light on.

HOW DOES THE SLOW COOKER WORK?

Most slow cookers have the same basic design —a dishwasher-safe stoneware insert, called the "container" or "crock," which sits inside a thin metal casing that houses the electrical element, and a lid. As the condensation accumulates inside the slow cooker it creates a low-pressure seal between the lid and the container. You can observe this when cooking after a long period of time, as water sputters around the edge of the lid. The electrical elements are encased in the side as well as the base, providing all-around heat.

WHICH SLOW COOKER TO BUY?

You have to do your research carefully before buying, as there are many brands and most vary from each other in a variety of ways. There are no industry standards; consequently, slow cookers cook at different temperatures, come in many sizes and can be round or oval.

You also have a wide choice of colors and decorative features. If you like entertaining, you will even find models that do double duty as a hostess cart, with space for keeping up to three dishes warm.

Yet, aesthetics are not the primary consideration when buying a slow cooker. The number of people you cook for and the type of food you like eating should ultimately determine which slow cooker you buy. The chart below lists some of the sizes available and their different capabilities.

WHICH SLOW COOKER TO BUY?

SIZE	SERVES	ROUND	OVAL
1½ quarts	1 to 2	Casseroles and stews, soups, single lamb shanks, stewed fruit, compotes, half quantities of most of the recipes in this book	
4 quarts	4 to 6	Casseroles and stews, soups, 4 lamb shanks, small ham roasts, stewed fruit, compotes, desserts cooked in round containers up to 4 cups, whole quantities of all the recipes in the book; not suitable for whole, large chickens and some roasts	Casseroles and stews, soups, 4 lamb shanks, small ham roasts, stewed fruit, compotes, desserts cooked in round containers up to 4 cups, small chickens and roasts, desserts cooked in a 2-cup bread pan, whole quantities of all the recipes in this book
5 quarts	6 to 8	Casseroles and stews, soups, 4 lamb shanks, small ham roasts, stewed fruit, compotes, desserts cooked in round containers up to 4 cups, whole quantities of all the recipes in this book	Casseroles and stews, soups, 4 lamb shanks, small ham roasts, stewed fruit, compotes, desserts cooked in round containers up to 4 cups, small and medium chickens, roasts, desserts cooked in a 3-cup bread pan, whole quantities of all the recipes in this book
6 quarts	8+	Casseroles and stews, soups, 6 lamb shanks, ham roasts, stewed fruit, compotes, desserts cooked in round containers up to 5 cups, large poultry and medium roasts, if they are rolled, whole quantities of all the recipes in this book, double quantities of the curry, casserole and stew recipes	Casseroles and stews, soups, 6 lamb shanks, small ham roasts, stewed fruit, compotes, desserts cooked in round containers up to 5 cups, most poultry and roasts, whole quantities of all the recipes in this book, double quantities of the curry, casserole, soup and stew recipes

As a general rule, the more modern your slow cooker is, the faster it will cook. Consequently, if you're using a slow cooker that's several years old to make the recipes in this book, you will need to adjust the cooking times accordingly.

Which features to look for? Once you have decided what size and shape slow cooker is most suitable for your requirements, there are other options to consider before buying. One quick way to research is to look at manufacturers' websites to compare models and features. This will also give you access to many users' manuals, some of which specify temperatures for different settings, but unfortunately, not always.

Manual or digital slow cooker? The most basic slow cookers have an On/Off switch and HIGH and LOW settings that you select manually. Some models also include an AUTO setting that cooks food on HIGH for one hour before automatically switching the temperature to LOW. Manual slow cookers are an economical option for anyone who is at home all the time and able to monitor the cooking process.

Slightly more expensive digital models, however, give you substantially more flexibility with programmable timings. If, for example, you aren't ready to eat when the cooking is complete, most digital models automatically switch to WARM, keeping the food hot until required. I think this is the most important feature, and essential for anyone who wants to put the ingredients in the cooker in the morning and come home to a warm meal that hasn't been overcooked into mush. The WARM function is also ideal for households where not everyone is eating at the same time, and can be used to keep some conventionally cooked foods, such as soups and stews, warm until it is time to serve. The WARM setting, however, should never be used to cook food.

Some digital slow cookers also have a SIMMER function, with a temperature that sits between LOW and WARM, for simmering soups.

The most sophisticated digital slow cookers come with a digital probe and are particularly good for cooking poultry and large roasts. These models cook according to temperature, rather than time, automatically switching to WARM when a specified internal temperature is reached.

Be sure to check how much flexibility a specific model offers before buying. My favorite slow cooker, for example, allows me to set the HIGH or LOW settings for up to 24 hours, and the WARM function keeps food hot for 8 hours, while other models have shorter settings.

Digital slow cookers also have an LCD display panel that counts down so you can see at a glance how much cooking time is left.

Is preheating required? Some manufacturers specify to preheat the empty slow cooker 20 minutes before adding any ingredients. Think about if this will be convenient for you or not. Many of the recipes in this book don't specify preheating because they were tested in a slow cooker that doesn't require it, but consult your slow cooker's manual before using any of the recipes and preheat the cooker if required.

Glass lids Although not essential, I favor a glass see-though lid, rather than a solid ceramic one, so I can monitor how the condensation is building up in the container. Because slow cookers make very little noise and give off fewer aromas than other methods of cooking, it can be reassuring to confirm by sight that the dish is progressing.

From cooker to table The early generation of slow cookers did not have removable porcelain, ceramic or dishwasher-safe containers, but this is a standard feature of modern cookers. To reduce the amount of washing up, buy a slow cooker with a container you are happy to serve from at the table.

The containers become very hot, so make sure the handles on the sides are large enough for you to easily lift it out of the metal casing. You will need to use oven mitts or a folded dish towel when you remove it, and you'll need a heatproof mat to put the hot container on.

Some larger models come with heatproof containers that are also safe to use on the stovetop, which also saves on the dishwashing.

Portability If you take meals to the elderly or ill, or just like sharing food with friends, consider one of the slow cooker models that comes with a securely locking lid so you can transport the container without spillages. Some models also have insulated bags for transporting the slow cooker with hot food inside, so it arrives hot and ready to eat.

Long cords Think about where the electrical socket you will be using is located and make sure the slow cooker has a long enough cord. As with all electrical appliances, the cord should not be near electric rings on the stovetop or gas flames, nor should it be too close to the sink. The outside of a slow cooker becomes very hot, so place it out of reach of children and somewhere you are unlikely to burn yourself.

HOW TO USE YOUR SLOW COOKER

Cooking in a slow cooker is both similar to and different from conventional cooking. The significant change required to your cooking technique is not to lift the lid before the end of the specified cooking time, unless instructed to in a recipe. Lifting the lid breaks the seal and lowers the temperature. Getting used to not lifting the lid is challenging when first using a slow cooker, as a cook's natural inclination is to sniff, stir and taste, but you must resist. If you do lift the lid, however, add 15 minutes to the total cooking time.

Although slow cookers don't require much attention once you switch them on, a certain amount of precooking preparation is necessary, and this can take as much time as if you are preparing, say, a stew conventionally on the stovetop. I think

it is a misconception about cooking in a slow cooker that you always just throw all the ingredients in, switch it on and walk out the door. Although some recipes follow that brief—and I've included a selection of them in this book—for the best results, the majority require your attention to get them started.

Since the heat in a slow cooker builds up from the bottom, put the densest ingredients, such as chopped root vegetables, in the cooker first and then add the meat and liquids.

If, like me, you aren't really interested in cooking your evening meal while eating breakfast, there are several techniques to get around this problem. Sometimes I cook really slow-cooking recipes, like Tuscan Lamb Shanks & Butter Beans (see page 77), overnight and transfer them to a conventional casserole or saucepan in the morning, ready for reheating that evening. More often, however, I do all the chopping and initial frying the night before so in the morning I really can put everything in the slow cooker, switch it on and walk out the door.

The most basic guideline of conventional cooking, however, also applies to cooking in a slow cooker: what you put in a slow cooker determines what you get out. Even though slow cookers are adept at transforming tough, inexpensive cuts of meat into tender meals, you can't use poor-quality ingredients and expect a good outcome. Always use good-quality meat, seafood and fruit and vegetables for the most satisfying results.

Adding liquids Many old-fashioned slow-cooker recipes specify to cover all the ingredients with liquid before covering with the lid and beginning the cooking process, but this isn't necessary. Recipes cooked in a slow cooker require *much* less liquid than those cooked on the stovetop or in the oven, because less evaporation takes place. This means the liquid that cooks out of any ingredients stays in the container. It is this liquid and any added liquid that creates the condensation, and if you have a glass lid you will see this building up and dropping from the lid back down onto the ingredients. Resist the temptation to add more liquid than specified in recipes until you are familiar with how your slow cooker operates.

You'll see many of the recipes in this book specify very small amounts of liquid. In Greek Spiced Beef & Onion Stew (see page 82), for example, the cubes of stewing beef cook in just the liquid from 1 pound grated tomatoes, 4 tablespoons dissolved tomato paste and 2 tablespoons red wine vinegar to produce a rich, thick stew.

Boosting the flavors Because of the condensation that collects in the slow cooker, flavors actually become diluted, not concentrated as you will often read. You need to add more herbs and spices than in conventional cooking to avoid insipid food. If your favorite conventional casserole recipe, for example, includes 1 crushed garlic clove, think about using 2 to 4 if you cook it in a slow cooker. I appreciate that sounds like an overpowering amount, but after a stew has simmered for eight hours the flavors will have mellowed.

Dry herbs, rather than fresh, are used in most slow-cooker recipes because the fresh ones simply lose their potency after long, slow cooking. Add fresh herbs at the end or sprinkled over the finished dish when their flavors can be appreciated. Some recipes specify to add dry herbs loose and these will be present in the finished dish, while a few specify to tie them in a piece of cheesecloth so they can be removed at the end of cooking.

Cooking poultry Whole chicken and poultry portions cook quickly and easily in slow cookers. To avoid any possibility of salmonella poisoning, my recipes specify to cook chicken and turkey dishes on the HIGH setting. I also suggest you don't leave cooked poultry dishes for a long time on the WARM setting.

Chicken skin can be given an appetizing golden color by browning it before adding to the slow cooker but it will lose its crispness. If you find this unappealing, remove the skin from the chicken before you add the pieces to the container.

Cooking beans and legumes Dry and soaked beans and legumes should be covered with liquid while they cook. If necessary, add extra boiling stock or other liquid before you switch the slow cooker on so they are just submerged. It isn't necessary for drained and rinsed canned beans and legumes to be covered with liquid.

Cooking rice Easy-cook white or brown rice is the best choice for cooking in a slow cooker. This rice has been parboiled and gives you tender, separate grains when cooked in a slow cooker. If you try other ordinary long-grain rice it becomes too sticky to be enjoyable. The Pumpkin & Dolcelatte Rice recipe (see page 132), however, uses risotto rice because the desired result is thicker and creamier than many rice recipes.

Cooking vegetables The long, slow cooking process in a slow cooker is ideal for cooking root vegetables, because it brings out their natural sweetness. It is important, however, to cut vegetables to similar sizes so they cook uniformly. Vegetables are generally put in the bottom of the cooker, so they are usually sufficiently covered with liquid but this isn't always necessary. Recipes will specify if you should add extra liquid to make sure the vegetables are completely submerged.

Green vegetables, such as bok choy, kale and spinach leaves, are generally added at the end of cooking, to preserve both their texture and their flavor.

Always thaw frozen vegetables, such as peas, before adding them to the slow cooker. If you are adding canned vegetables, such as corn kernels, drain and rinse them well before adding.

Making stocks After the first time I made chicken stock in my slow cooker, it was obvious to me I probably wouldn't be making it again in the conventional manner. I simply put all the ingredients in the cooker and switched it on before I went to bed. In the morning I had a container full of delicious stock, ready for cooling and freezing. Nothing could have been easier.

I always think that when I go to the trouble of making fresh stock I might as well make more than I need, so I always have a good frozen supply. All the stock recipes in this book (see pages 168–169) are ready to use as soon as they have finished cooking, or they can be left to cool completely and then chilled up to two days, or frozen up to three months. The exception is the fish stock, which is best used within a day.

Frying ingredients Some recipes specify to fry ingredients before adding them to the slow cooker. This is to give meat a good color, start the cooking process for vegetables and enhance the flavor of alliums, such as garlic and onions. Also, raw spices such as ground coriander and cumin, need to be fried briefly to cook out the "raw" flavor. Even if a dish cooks for eight or ten hours in a slow cooker, spices will still taste "raw" if they aren't fried first.

Many cooks prefer to cut the preparation time by not frying meat before adding it to the cooker. I usually find the texture at the end of cooking, however, less appetizing, although several of my recipes do skip this step and still manage to work well. Be sure to pat meat dry before frying, and cook in batches, if necessary, to avoid overcrowding the pan. When the pan is too full, the temperature drops and the meat steams, rather than fries. Browning fatty ingredients, such as chorizo, before adding to the slow cooker helps to eliminate excessive fat from the finished dish.

Covering food during cooking Because of the condensation that builds up and then drips down off the lid, it is necessary to cover certain dishes with foil or plastic wrap while they cook, especially desserts, to prevent them becoming soggy. Cover tightly with plastic wrap or foil, molded over the top of the dish. When you are cooking something surrounded by boiling water, such as Almond Crème Caramel (see page 159), be sure not to let the plastic wrap or foil extend down to the water level, or steam will seep underneath.

Skimming fat To make the finished dish more appetizing, I think it's important to skim fat from the surface of dishes when they finish cooking, especially when they are made with fatty meat cuts, such as pork belly, chorizo or lamb shanks.

Thickening cooking juices Again, because of the condensation in the slow cooker, sauces tend to be very thin and watery. Recipes compensate for this by using much less liquid than in conventional recipes (see page 10), but there are additional ways to create richer, thicker sauces.

Meat can be dusted with all-purpose flour or cornstarch before browning, which dissolves into the liquid and thickens the juices during the cooking process. Cornstarch or arrowroot dissolved in a few tablespoons of cold water can be stirred into the slow cooker and then cooked on HIGH until the cooking liquid thickens.

A NOTE ABOUT COOKING TIMES

It is difficult to give accurate cooking times because the cooking temperatures of different brands vary. As a general rule of thumb, older cookers have lower temperatures than modern ones, and smaller cookers cook faster than larger ones.

I also don't give a range of cooking times, but after you've made several of the recipes in this book, you will know if you have to cook for longer or shorter times.

All the recipes in this book have been tested in a 4-quart oval slow cooker with a HIGH temperature of 212°F and a LOW temperature of 199°F. Consult your users' manual to see if your cooker's specifications differ, and compare the cooking time in similar recipes to determine if you should cook recipes for longer or shorter times. It is, unfortunately, a matter of trial and error.

If you've lost the users' manual that came with your slow cooker, use this simple test to determine if it is hotter or cooler than the one used for recipe testing. Measure 4 cups water into a large measuring jug and leave to sit on the counter for several hours so it comes to room temperature. Pour it into the slow cooker, cover and switch to HIGH. The water in mine boils after 1½ hours.

THE BEST MEATS TO USE

As with casseroles cooked the conventional way, the least expensive cuts of meat with tough connective tissues are ideal for using in slow cookers. The slow cooking process breaks down the tissues for tender results. I like to make casseroles and stews with 2-inch pieces of meat. The chart below lists the best meat cuts to use.

ENJOY YOUR SLOW COOKER

My conversion to the benefits of using a slow cooker happened one afternoon while I was sitting on a bus stuck in a traffic jam and a beef stew was simmering away at home. It was with a sense of relief that I realized dinner would not be ruined, regardless of how late I was getting home. I knew my slow cooker would automatically switch itself to its WARM setting at the end of the programmed cooking time.

It was, however, a rocky road to conversion. The first recipes I tried were insipid and bland. I regularly complained about eating "food without soul." It wasn't until I decided to tear up the rule book and develop my own recipes that I started to really enjoy slow-cooker meals. This collection of recipes is the result of my trials and errors. I made many common mistakes, like adding too much liquid or not enough flavorings, but as I tried and tested, I developed recipes with rich, succulent flavors.

I have tried to push the boundaries of a slow cooker book to give you recipes that are more than just home-comfort meals, but ones that you could make for friends coming around for dinner or for special occasions.

Each recipe shows the time it takes to cook, and a star symbol on some of the recipes indicates whether it's a super-easy recipe. Whatever the occasion, I hope you find the inspiration you've always wanted in a cookbook for getting the most out of your slow cooker. I also hope this collection of recipes inspires you to try some new ingredients and flavor combinations.

THE BEST MEAT CUTS TO USE

Beef	brisket, bone-in short ribs, boneless chuck (shoulder), boneless leg, flank steak, ground beef, ox cheeks, oxtail, shin, silverside, skirt steak
Lamb	boneless leg, boneless shoulder, shank
Pork	boneless leg, boneless pork steaks, boneless shoulder, ham hock, ham knuckle, ham roasts, pork belly, sausages
Veal	boneless shoulder, osso buco (cross-cut shank)

All the recipes in this book have been tested in a 4-quart oval slow cooker with a HIGH temperature of 212°F and a LOW temperature of 199°F. Cooking times will vary in models with different specifications.

 You'll find this symbol whenever a recipe is super-easy to make. This means there is minimal or no prepping involved. You just add the ingredients and switch on the slow cooker.

SOUPS & SAUCES

The most difficult part about writing this chapter was choosing the recipes to include. The list was long, because a slow cooker is ideal for making soups and sauces: they don't require any attention while they cook and it's virtually impossible for them to scorch and burn. That's a real bonus with the sauce recipes, especially one like Barbecue Sauce (see page 33), with its high sugar content.

I also particularly appreciated the versatility of my slow cooker when I was testing soup recipes at the height of a heat wave and the kitchen wasn't full of steam—it really is a kitchen appliance for the whole year around.

This chapter contains a selection of quick-cooking soups, such as Chicken, Vegetable & Barley Broth (see page 16), as well as soups you can put on in the morning in anticipation of your evening meal. If you want a pot of warming soup waiting for you when you walk through the door after a long day, try German Lentil Soup (see page 22). Vegetarians will also find a good selection of suitable recipes in this chapter, such as the Split Pea, Celery Root & Spinach Soup (see page 23) and the Red Lentil & Sweet Potato Soup (see page 27).

When I go to the effort of making a homemade sauce I can't see the point of making enough for just one meal. I love using my slow cooker for making hassle-free sauces in larger quantities, so I always have a supply in the freezer. And, again, because the pot doesn't dry out, I just go about my day's activities without giving the simmering sauce a second thought.

◀ CHINESE HOTPOT (SEE PAGE 27)

CHICKEN, VEGETABLE & BARLEY BROTH

PREPARATION TIME: 20 minutes, plus making the stock (optional)
COOKING TIME: 2½ hours on HIGH   **SERVES 4**

2 cups diced mixed root vegetables, such as carrot, celery root, parsnip, rutabaga and turnip, diced

1 celery stick, thinly sliced

1 leek, halved lengthwise, thinly sliced and rinsed

2 bay leaves, tied together with 1 small bunch of parsley sprigs with crushed stalks

2 chicken quarters, skins removed

2 tablespoons pot barley

4½ cups Chicken Stock (see page 168) or store-bought stock, boiling, plus extra if needed

salt and freshly ground black pepper

snipped chives or chopped parsley leaves, to serve

Put the root vegetables, celery, leek and herb bundle in the slow cooker. Add the chicken quarters and barley, tucking the barley down between the chicken pieces. Pour the stock over, adding extra to cover the barley, if necessary, and season with salt and pepper.

Cover the cooker with the lid. Cook on HIGH 2 hours until the juices from the chicken run clear when the thickest part of the meat is pierced with the tip of a sharp knife or skewer. Remove the chicken from the cooker and leave to rest about 10 minutes. Meanwhile, re-cover the cooker and cook 30 minutes longer until the vegetables and barley are tender.

When the chicken is cool enough to handle, remove the meat from the bones and cut into bite-size pieces. Wrap in foil and keep warm.

When the vegetables and barley are tender, return the chicken to the cooker and heat through, if necessary. Remove and discard the herb bundle and add a little more salt and pepper, if you like. Sprinkle with chives and serve.

TURKEY, WILD RICE & TOMATO SOUP

PREPARATION TIME: 20 minutes, plus making the stock (optional)
COOKING TIME: 2 hours on HIGH   **SERVES 4**

14 ounces boneless, skinless turkey breast

turkey bones (optional)

1 tablespoon dry basil or dry tarragon

½ cup wild rice

1 tablespoon sunflower oil

1 onion, finely chopped

2 garlic cloves, finely chopped

3 cups Vegetable Stock (see page 169), Chicken Stock (see page 168) or store-bought stock

1¼ cups tomato puree

salt and freshly ground black pepper

shredded basil leaves or chopped tarragon leaves, to serve

crusty bread, to serve (optional)

Season the turkey breast with salt and pepper. Put the turkey in the slow cooker with any bones, if using, and sprinkle the dry basil over. Add the rice, tucking it down around the meat.

Heat the oil in a large skillet over high heat. Lower the heat to medium, add the onion and fry, stirring, 2 minutes. Add the garlic and fry 1 to 3 minutes longer until the onion is soft.

Add the stock and tomato puree and season lightly with salt and pepper. Bring to a boil, then pour the mixture into the cooker.

Cover the cooker with the lid. Cook on HIGH 2 hours until the rice is fluffy and tender and the juices from the turkey run clear when the thickest part of the meat is pierced with the tip of a sharp knife or skewer. Remove and discard the bones, if necessary. Remove the turkey from the cooker and leave to cool slightly. Re-cover the cooker to keep the rice warm.

When the turkey is cool enough to handle, cut into bite-size pieces, then return it to the cooker and heat through, if necessary. Add a little more salt and pepper, if you like. Sprinkle with basil and serve with crusty bread, if you like.

VARIATIONS
For a spicier soup, add 1 tablespoon curry paste with the garlic. The soup is also good with shredded kale. When you remove the turkey, wrap it in foil and keep warm, then stir in the kale and cook 15 minutes on HIGH until it is tender. Return the chopped turkey to the cooker to heat through.

HOT & SOUR DUCK & MUSHROOM SOUP

PREPARATION TIME: 15 minutes, plus making the stock (optional)
COOKING TIME: 3 hours on LOW, plus 20 minutes on HIGH **SERVES 4**

½ ounce dry Asian mushrooms, such as oyster or cloud ear

2 duck legs, about 9 ounces each, skins and fat removed

6 Thai shallots or 3 large French shallots, halved

1 dry red Thai chili, seeded if you like, and halved

1½ teaspoons sugar

4 cups Vegetable Stock (see page 169) or water

2 tablespoons fish sauce, plus extra to taste

1 tablespoon lemon juice, plus extra to taste

1 tablespoon arrowroot or cornstarch

1 cup bean sprouts

salt and freshly ground black pepper

cilantro leaves or Thai basil leaves, to serve

Put the dry mushrooms in a strainer and rinse under cold running water to remove any dirt.

Put the duck legs, mushrooms, shallots, chili and sugar in the slow cooker. Pour the stock, fish sauce and lemon juice over, stirring to dissolve the sugar. Season with salt and pepper.

Cover the cooker with the lid. Cook on LOW 3 hours until the juices from the duck run clear when the thickest part of the meat is pierced with the tip of a sharp knife or skewer. Remove the duck from the cooker and leave to rest about 10 minutes.

Meanwhile, remove the shallots and chili and discard. Put the arrowroot and 2 tablespoons cold water in a small bowl and stir until smooth, then stir the paste into the cooking liquid. Switch the cooker to HIGH, re-cover and cook 15 minutes until the soup thickens slightly.

When the duck is cool enough to handle, remove all the meat from the bones and cut into thin pieces. When the soup has thickened, return the duck to the cooker with the bean sprouts and stir to heat through. Add a little more fish sauce, lemon juice and salt and pepper, if you like. Sprinkle with cilantro and serve.

COOK'S TIP
Use a small knife to carefully remove the skin and fat from the duck legs—the legs are slippery and difficult to handle so it helps if you dust your fingers with salt first.

GERMAN LENTIL SOUP

If you've never added a splash of vinegar to a bowlful of lentil soup, give it a try.
Stirring in as little as half a teaspoon per serving really lifts the flavor.

PREPARATION TIME: 15 minutes
COOKING TIME: 6 hours on LOW, plus 30 minutes on HIGH   **SERVES 4**

1 tablespoon sunflower oil, plus extra if needed

½ cup smoked lardons or thick smoked back bacon, sliced

2 carrots, diced

1 onion, finely chopped

½ celery stick, finely chopped

1 cup dry brown lentils, rinsed

1 floury potato, such as Yukon Gold, finely chopped

2 bay leaves

1 tablespoon dry parsley

1 tablespoon dry thyme

4 smoked or plain frankfurters, cut into bite-size pieces

salt and freshly ground black pepper

2 teaspoons red wine vinegar or white wine vinegar or to taste, to serve

chopped parsley leaves, to serve

dark rye bread (optional), to serve

Heat the oil in a large skillet over high heat. Lower the heat to low, add the lardons and fry 1 to 2 minutes until they give off their fat and start to crisp. Use a slotted spoon to transfer the lardons to the slow cooker.

Add the carrots, onion and celery to the pan, adding extra oil if necessary, and fry, stirring, 3 to 5 minutes until the onion is soft. Transfer the vegetables to the cooker, then add the lentils, potato, bay leaves, dry parsley and thyme and season with pepper. Pour 4 cups boiling water over, or enough to cover the lentils.

Cover the cooker with the lid and cook on LOW 6 hours until the lentils and potato are almost tender. Remove and discard the bay leaves. Season with salt and a little more pepper, if you like, and stir in the frankfurters.

Switch the cooker to HIGH, re-cover and cook 30 minutes until the frankfurters are hot. Stir in the vinegar, sprinkle with parsley and serve with dark rye bread, if you like.

SPLIT PEA, CELERY ROOT & SPINACH SOUP

PREPARATION TIME: 20 minutes, plus making the stock (optional)
COOKING TIME: 5 hours 20 minutes on HIGH   **SERVES 4**

1¼ cups dry green split peas, rinsed

½ cup peeled and diced celery root

2 garlic cloves, chopped

1 bay leaf

1 onion, chopped

5 cups Vegetable Stock (see page 169), Chicken Stock (see page 168) or store-bought stock, boiling, plus extra if needed

1 tablespoon white wine vinegar

7 ounces baby spinach leaves

4 smoked bacon or cured bacon slices (optional)

salt and freshly ground black pepper

finely chopped dill or parsley leaves, to serve

Put the split peas, celery root, garlic, bay leaf and onion in the slow cooker. Pour the stock over, adding extra to cover the split peas, if necessary, and season with pepper.

Cover the cooker with the lid and cook on HIGH 5 hours until the split peas are dissolving and the celery root is very tender. Stir in the vinegar and add the spinach, using a spoon to push it into the soup. Cook, uncovered, 10 to 15 minutes longer, stirring once, until the spinach is tender. Season with salt and a little more pepper, if you like.

Strain the soup, reserving the cooking liquid. Remove and discard the bay leaf. Puree the split peas, celery root and spinach in a blender or food processor until smooth, then return the mixture to the cooker and slowly stir in the reserved liquid until the desired consistency is achieved. Re-cover the cooker to keep the soup warm.

Meanwhile, for the bacon, if using, heat the broiler to high. When hot, broil the bacon 2 to 3 minutes on each side until cooked and crisp. Drain well on paper towels, then finely chop. Sprinkle the soup with the bacon and dill and serve.

VARIATION
For a vegetarian version, omit the bacon and sprinkle the soup with toasted pumpkin or sunflower seeds for texture and crumbled feta cheese for richness.

(10)

SMOKY & SPICY BLACK BEAN SOUP

PREPARATION TIME: 30 minutes, plus making the stock and tortilla chips (optional)
COOKING TIME: 10 hours on LOW   **SERVES 4**

2 tablespoons olive oil

½ cup chopped smoked bacon

1 large onion, finely chopped

4 large garlic cloves, finely chopped

1 tablespoon ground cumin

2 teaspoons ground coriander

½ teaspoon ground cloves

¼ teaspoon cayenne pepper

3½ cups Chicken Stock (see page 168), Vegetable Stock (see page 169) or store-bought stock, plus extra if needed

1¼ cups dry black beans

2 tablespoons dry oregano

1 tablespoon dry thyme

1 dry chipotle chili pepper, seeded if you like

1 avocado

1 tablespoon lime juice

salt and freshly ground black pepper

feta cheese, drained and crumbled, to serve

cherry tomatoes, seeded and chopped, to serve

chopped cilantro leaves, to serve

lime wedges, to serve

Tortilla Chips (see page 174) or shop-bought tortilla chips, to serve

ADDITIONAL TOPPINGS (OPTIONAL)

hard-boiled eggs, shelled and finely chopped

scallions, finely chopped

sour cream

Heat 1 tablespoon of the oil in a large saucepan over high heat. Lower the heat to low, add the bacon and fry 1 to 2 minutes until it gives off its fat and starts to crisp. Use a slotted spoon to transfer the bacon to the slow cooker.

Pour off any excess fat from the pan, leaving about 1 tablespoon. Add the onion and fry, stirring, 2 minutes. Add the garlic, cumin, coriander, cloves and cayenne pepper and fry 1 to 3 minutes longer until the onion is soft.

Add the stock, beans, oregano, thyme and chipotle chili and season with pepper. Bring to a boil and boil vigorously 10 minutes. Pour the bean mixture into the cooker and add extra stock to just cover the beans, if necessary.

Cover the cooker with the lid and cook on LOW 10 hours until the beans are very tender. Remove and discard the chipotle chili.

Transfer half of the beans and liquid to a blender or food processor and puree, or mash in a bowl. Return the mixture to the cooker and stir into the soup. Season with salt and a little more pepper.

Pit, peel and finely chop the avocado, then toss with the lime juice. Divide the soup into bowls, top with the avocado, feta cheese and tomatoes and sprinkle with cilantro. Serve with lime wedges for squeezing over, tortilla chips and a selection of additional toppings, if you like.

CHINESE HOTPOT

PREPARATION TIME: 10 minutes,
  plus making the stock (optional)
COOKING TIME: 9½ hours on LOW,
  plus 30 minutes on HIGH   **SERVES 4**

1 pound 2 ounces beef flank seak
2½ cups Beef Stock (see page 168)
  or store-bought stock
½ cup Chinese rice wine
3 garlic cloves, crushed
1 star anise
2 teaspoons chili bean paste
2 teaspoons sugar
1½ teaspoons ground cumin
1 tablespoon soy sauce
a pinch Szechuan pepper
5 ounces thin Chinese egg noodles
1-inch piece gingerroot
1 teaspoon toasted sesame oil
4 scallions, finely chopped, to serve
chopped cilantro leaves, to serve

Put the beef, stock, rice wine, garlic, star anise, chili bean paste, sugar, cumin, soy sauce and Szechuan pepper in the slow cooker, stirring to dissolve the chili bean paste.

Cover the cooker and cook on LOW 9½ hours until the beef is very tender. Remove the beef from the cooker, wrap in foil and leave 10 minutes. Meanwhile, switch the cooker to HIGH, re-cover and heat 15 minutes. Stir in the noodles, re-cover and cook 15 minutes longer until they are tender.

When the beef has rested, shred the meat, then re-wrap and keep warm. When the noodles are cooked, stir in the beef, then grate the ginger directly into the broth and add the sesame oil. Sprinkle with scallions and cilantro and serve.

RED LENTIL & SWEET POTATO SOUP

PREPARATION TIME: 15 minutes,
  plus making the stock (optional)
COOKING TIME: 3 hours on HIGH   **SERVES 4**

1 large red onion, finely chopped
4 large garlic cloves, finely chopped
a pinch red pepper flakes
1½ cups peeled and diced sweet potatoes
1 red bell pepper, halved lengthwise, seeded and
  quartered
¾ cup red lentils, rinsed
4 cups Vegetable Stock (see page 169) or store-bought
  stock, boiling, plus extra if needed
1 tablespoon olive oil
2 teaspoons balsamic vinegar
salt and freshly ground black pepper
chopped parsley leaves, to serve

Put all the ingredients, except the balsamic vinegar, in the slow cooker and season with pepper. Add extra stock to cover the lentils, if necessary.

Cover the cooker with the lid and cook on HIGH 3 hours until the lentils and sweet potato are tender.

Remove the pepper pieces and discard. Stir well and season with salt and a little more pepper, if you like. Stir in the balsamic vinegar, sprinkle with parsley and serve.

SUMMER TOMATO SOUP

PREPARATION TIME: 15 minutes, plus making
the stock (optional)
COOKING TIME: 2½ hours on HIGH,
plus 5½ hours on LOW   **SERVES 4**

4 large garlic cloves, chopped
2 celery sticks, chopped
1 large red onion, chopped
3½ pounds juicy tomatoes, peeled, seeded and
chopped
2 bay leaves
1 tablespoon dry parsley
1 teaspoon sugar
½ cup Vegetable Stock (see page 169) or store-bought
stock, plus extra if needed
salt and freshly ground black pepper
4 tablespoons crème fraîche or sour cream, to serve

Put the garlic, celery and red onion in the slow
cooker. Add the tomatoes, bay leaves, parsley,
sugar and stock, then season with salt and pepper.

Cover the cooker with the lid and cook on HIGH
2½ hours. Stir the tomatoes well. Switch the cooker
to LOW, re-cover and cook 5½ hours longer until
the tomatoes break down and the vegetables are
tender. Remove and discard the bay leaves.

Strain the soup into a bowl, pressing down to extract
as much liquid as possible. Reserve the cooking
liquid. Puree the tomato mixture in a blender
or food processor until smooth, then return the
mixture to the cooker and slowly stir in the reserved
cooking liquid and extra stock, if necessary, until the
desired consistency is achieved. Add a little more salt
and pepper, if you like. Serve hot or chilled, with a
dollop of crème fraîche.

SPICED SQUASH & APPLE SOUP

▶

PREPARATION TIME: 15 minutes, plus making
the stock and cream (optional)
COOKING TIME: 12 hours on LOW   **SERVES 4**

3 cups peeled, seeded butternut squash cut into
½-inch pieces
1-inch piece gingerroot, peeled and chopped
2 bay leaves, torn
2 cinnamon sticks
2 large garlic cloves, finely chopped
1 Granny Smith apple, peeled, cored and chopped
1 leek, halved lengthwise, finely chopped and rinsed
1 teaspoon ground coriander
⅛ teaspoon cayenne pepper, or to taste
4 cups Vegetable Stock (see page 169) or
store-bought stock
2 tablespoons apple juice
salt and freshly ground black pepper
finely chopped parsley leaves, to serve
sunflower seeds, to serve
1 recipe quantity Maple Cream (see page 171),
to serve (optional)

Put the squash, ginger, bay leaves, cinnamon sticks,
garlic, apple, leek, coriander and cayenne pepper
in the slow cooker. Season with salt and pepper,
then pour over the stock.

Cover the cooker with the lid and cook on LOW
12 hours until the squash is very tender and the
flavors are blended. Remove and discard the bay
leaves and cinnamon sticks. Puree the soup
in a blender or food processor until smooth. Stir
in the apple juice and add a little more salt and
pepper, if you like. Sprinkle with parsley and
sunflower seeds and serve with a swirl of Maple
Cream, if you like.

MINESTRONE

This soup is full of fresh Mediterranean flavors. You can make it in advance and reheat it, but only add the thin pasta pieces just before serving or they become overcooked and mushy if left to sit too long in the hot broth.

PREPARATION TIME: 25 minutes, plus 8 hours soaking the beans, making the stock and sauce (optional)
COOKING TIME: 3¼ hours on HIGH   **SERVES 4**

1 cup dry cannellini beans, soaked in cold water at least 8 hours

1½ cups diced zucchini

1½ cups finely chopped thin green beans

4 large garlic cloves, finely chopped

1 onion, finely chopped

1 celery stick, finely chopped

1 carrot, diced

1 leek, halved lengthwise, thinly sliced and rinsed

3½ cups Vegetable Stock (see page 169), store-bought stock or water, boiling, plus extra if needed

⅔ cup tomato puree

1 tablespoon extra virgin olive oil, plus extra to serve

2 bay leaves, tied together with several rosemary and thyme sprigs

½ teaspoon sugar

4 large tomatoes

2 ounces dry angel hair pasta, broken up

salt and freshly ground black pepper

freshly grated Parmesan cheese, to serve

1 recipe quantity Pesto Sauce (see page 171) or 4 tablespoons store-bought fresh pesto, to serve

Bring a large, covered saucepan of unsalted water to a boil. Drain the beans and add them to the pan. Return the water to the boil and boil vigorously 10 minutes. Drain and rinse the beans, then transfer them to the slow cooker.

Add all of the remaining ingredients, except the tomatoes and pasta, and season with pepper. Add extra stock to cover the beans, if necessary.

Cover the cooker with the lid and cook on HIGH 3 hours until the beans are tender.

Meanwhile, use a sharp knife to cut a cross in the bottom of each tomato, then put them in a heatproof bowl and cover with boiling water. Leave to stand 2 to 3 minutes, then drain. Peel off and discard the skins, then seed and dice.

When the beans are tender, stir in the tomatoes and pasta and season with salt. Re-cover the cooker and cook 15 minutes longer until the pasta is tender. Remove and discard the herb bundle and add a little more salt and pepper, if you like. Sprinkle with Parmesan, add a splash of olive oil and serve with a dollop of Pesto Sauce.

RUSTIC ITALIAN BEAN SOUP

The oil-rich Garlic Croutons (see page 170) add texture and flavor to this simple soup. If you don't have time to make any, serve the soup with slices of toasted ciabatta bread instead.

PREPARATION TIME: 25 minutes, plus 8 hours soaking the beans, making the stock and croutons (optional)
COOKING TIME: 2½ hours on HIGH **SERVES 4**

1 cup dry cannellini beans, soaked in cold water at least 8 hours

1 carrot, diced

2 celery sticks, finely chopped

4 garlic cloves, finely chopped

1 onion, halved, and each half studded with 2 cloves

1 tablespoon dry sage

5 cups Vegetable Stock (see page 169), store-bought stock or water, boiling, plus extra if needed

1 tablespoon extra virgin olive oil, plus extra, to serve

2 tablespoons finely chopped parsley leaves

salt and freshly ground black pepper

1 recipe quantity Garlic Croutons (see page 170), to serve (optional)

Bring a large, covered saucepan of unsalted water to a boil. Drain the beans and add them to the pan. Return to the boil and boil vigorously 10 minutes.

Meanwhile, put the carrot, celery, garlic, onion and sage in the slow cooker.

Drain and rinse the beans, then transfer them to the cooker. Pour the stock and oil over and season with pepper. Add extra stock to just cover the beans, if necessary.

Cover the cooker with the lid and cook on HIGH 2½ hours until the beans are very tender. Remove and discard the onion and any loose cloves.

Strain the soup into a large bowl, reserving the cooking liquid. Puree half of the beans with a little of the reserved liquid in a blender or food processor until smooth. Return the mixture and the remaining beans to the cooker and slowly stir in the remaining reserved cooking liquid until the desired consistency is achieved. Season with salt and a little more pepper, if you like, and stir in the parsley. Sprinkle with Garlic Croutons, if you like, drizzle with olive oil and serve.

APPLESAUCE

PREPARATION TIME: 15 minutes
COOKING TIME: 8 hours on LOW
MAKES ABOUT 2¼ pounds

3¼ pounds tart apples, peeled, quartered and cored
1 cinnamon stick (optional)
4 tablespoons sugar, plus extra to taste
finely grated zest of 1 lemon, plus extra to taste

Put the apples and cinnamon stick, if using, in the slow cooker and pour 4 cups water over. The apples will not be completely covered.

Cover the cooker with the lid and cook on LOW 8 hours until the apples are very tender. Remove and discard the cinnamon stick, if necessary.

Strain the sauce, reserving the cooking liquid (see Cook's Tip, below). Return the apples to the cooker and, using a potato masher or wooden spoon, mash to a texture as chunky as you like. Alternatively, process the sauce through a food mill until smooth, then return to the cooker.

Stir in the sugar and lemon zest, adding a little more sugar and zest, if you like, and stir until the sugar dissolves. Serve hot or chilled.

If not serving immediately, leave the sauce to cool completely, then cover and chill. Keep refrigerated up to 2 days, or freeze up to 1 month.

COOK'S TIP
This recipe is a great way to take advantage of windfall apples—abundant and inexpensive in the autumn. Don't waste the flavorsome cooking liquid. Leave it to cool and you'll have a delicious apple juice. Try it chilled over ice with a little gingerroot grated in.

BARBECUE SAUCE

PREPARATION TIME: 15 minutes, plus cooling
  and 24 hours chilling
COOKING TIME: 8 hours on LOW
MAKES ABOUT 3½ cups

2 tablespoons sunflower oil
2 celery sticks, finely chopped
2 onions, finely chopped
4 large garlic cloves, crushed
1½ cups apple cider vinegar
⅔ cup tomato paste
1 cup firmly packed soft light brown sugar
4 tablespoons dark molasses
4 tablespoons Worcestershire sauce
2 tablespoons Dijon mustard
4 teaspoons hot, smoked or sweet paprika
2 teaspoons celery seeds
½ teaspoon cayenne pepper
salt and freshly ground black pepper

Heat the oil in a saucepan over high heat. Lower the heat to medium, add the celery and onions and fry, stirring, 2 minutes. Add the garlic and fry 1 to 3 minutes longer until the onions are soft.

Add all of the remaining ingredients and stir until the sugar and molasses dissolve. Season with salt and pepper, then bring to a boil, stirring. Pour the sauce into the slow cooker, scraping the side of the pan with a rubber spatula.

Cover the cooker with the lid and cook on LOW 8 hours. Pour the sauce into a blender or food processor and blend until smooth. Add a little more salt and pepper, if you like. Leave the sauce to cool completely, then cover and chill 1 day to let the flavors blend. Serve hot or chilled. Keep any remaining sauce refrigerated up to 2 weeks, or freeze up to 1 month.

(6)

BOLOGNESE SAUCE

PREPARATION TIME: 30 minutes
COOKING TIME: 6 hours on LOW
MAKES ABOUT 2 pounds

2 tablespoons olive oil
1 ounce smoked pancetta or bacon, chopped
1 carrot, finely diced
1 celery stick, peeled and finely diced
1 onion, finely chopped
4 large garlic cloves, finely chopped
1 pound 2 ounces ground beef
4 tablespoons dry Italian herbs
2 tablespoons all-purpose flour
1 cup dry red wine
3 cups canned crushed tomatoes
4 tablespoons tomato puree
1½ teaspoons sugar
salt and freshly ground black pepper

Heat the oil in a skillet over high heat. Lower the heat to low, add the pancetta and fry, stirring, 1 to 2 minutes until it starts to crisp. Use a slotted spoon to transfer the pancetta to the slow cooker.

Pour off any excess fat from the pan, leaving about 2 tablespoons. Add the carrot, celery, onion and garlic and fry, stirring, 8 to 10 minutes. Increase the heat to medium. Add the beef and herbs and fry 2 to 3 minutes longer until brown. Stir in the flour and cook 2 minutes. Add the wine, increase the heat to high and leave to boil until it almost evaporates.

Transfer the meat mixture to the cooker and stir in the crushed tomatoes, tomato puree and sugar, and season lightly with salt and pepper. Cover the cooker and cook on LOW 6 hours, then serve.

If not serving immediately, leave the sauce to cool completely, then cover and chill. Keep refrigerated up to 3 days, or freeze up to 1 month.

(4)

EASY TOMATO SAUCE

PREPARATION TIME: 15 minutes
COOKING TIME: 4 hours on LOW
MAKES ABOUT 3 cups

5 tablespoons olive oil
2 onions, finely chopped
8 large garlic cloves, peeled
3 tablespoons dry Italian herbs
3½ pounds plum tomatoes
1 cup tomato puree
1½ teaspoons sugar
salt and freshly ground black pepper

Heat 4 tablespoons of the oil in a large skillet over high heat. Lower the heat to medium, add the onions and fry, stirring, 5 to 8 minutes until just starting to turn golden. Add the garlic and fry 1 minute longer.

Transfer the onions and garlic to the slow cooker and stir in the dry herbs. Add the plum tomatoes, tomato puree, sugar and the remaining oil and season with salt and pepper.

Cover the cooker with the lid and cook on LOW 4 hours until the tomatoes break down and the sauce is thick.

Smash the garlic into the side of the container or remove it, depending on how garlicky you like your sauce, and serve. Alternatively, transfer to a blender or food processor and puree until smooth before serving.

If not serving immediately, leave the sauce to cool completely, then cover and chill. Keep refrigerated up to 3 days, or freeze up to 1 month.

MEAT & POULTRY

This is the chapter where the slow cooker really comes into its own, and, consequently, I have devoted more than half the book to the subject. The recipes here are drawn from cuisines around the world, and the flavors range from hot and spicy curries through fruity tagines to mild-tasting turkey simmered in apple juice.

I've included recipes you can leave to cook all day, ready for the evening, as well as a selection of quicker ones, such as the rice-based dishes. I've also developed recipes that are a complete meal-in-a-pot, such as Massaman Beef & Potato Curry (see page 97), so when you lift the lid off your cooker there isn't anything to do but serve and enjoy.

To add dumplings to any of your slow cooker stews, use the recipe for Classic Beef Stew with Cheese & Herb Dumplings (see page 81) as a template. It is specifically cooked on the high setting so the liquid is hot enough for the dumplings to cook through and not become stodgy. The recipe also contains more stock than is specified in other recipes so the dumplings have plently of liquid to cook in.

If you're sceptical about cooking a whole chicken in a slow cooker, try the French "Roast" Lemon & Thyme Chicken (see page 48). The skin isn't as crisp as when roasted in the oven, but the lemon butter keeps the breasts wonderfully flavorful and moist.

This chapter might also introduce you to new inexpensive cuts of meat. If you've never tried ox cheeks or oxtails, for example, I urge you to. They appear so unpromising but the slow cooker miraculously tranforms them into tender, succulent meat.

◄ GREEK SPICED BEEF & ONION STEW (SEE PAGE 82)

CHICKEN JALFREZI

When I make the curry paste, I often make double the quantity and freeze the leftovers, saving even more time when I'm next in the mood for a spicy meal.

PREPARATION TIME: 25 minutes, plus making the curry paste and raita
COOKING TIME: 2 hours on HIGH   **SERVES 4**

2 pounds chicken thighs, skins removed

2 tablespoons ghee, peanut oil or sunflower oil

2 green bell peppers, halved lengthwise, seeded and sliced

2 red bell peppers, halved lengthwise, seeded and sliced

1 green chili, seeded if you like, and sliced

1 onion, thinly sliced

1 recipe quantity Jalfrezi Curry Paste (see page 170)

1 can (15-oz.) crushed tomatoes

a pinch garam masala

salt and freshly ground black pepper

cilantro leaves, to serve

1 recipe quantity Cucumber & Mint Raita or Cucumber & Tomato Raita (see page 172), to serve

cooked pilau or basmati rice, to serve

warm naan breads, to serve

Put the chicken in the slow cooker. Melt the ghee in a large skillet over high heat. Lower the heat to medium, add the peppers, chili and onion and fry, stirring, 6 to 8 minutes until the onion is soft and just starting to brown. Stir in the jalfrezi paste and fry 1 minute longer.

Add the crushed tomatoes and season with salt and pepper. Bring to a boil, stirring, then pour the mixture into the cooker.

Cover the cooker with the lid. Cook on HIGH 2 hours until the juices from the chicken run clear when the thickest part of the meat is pierced with the tip of a sharp knife or skewer.

Add a little more salt and pepper, if you like, and sprinkle the garam masala over. Sprinkle with cilantro and serve with Cucumber and Mint Raita, rice and naan breads.

CAJUN CHICKEN LIVER RICE

PREPARATION TIME: 25 minutes, plus making the stock (optional) and at least 5 minutes standing
COOKING TIME: 1½ hours on HIGH   **SERVES 4**

2 tablespoons sunflower oil, plus extra if needed

2 celery sticks, finely chopped

2 green bell peppers, halved lengthwise, seeded and finely chopped

1 onion, finely chopped

4 scallions, finely chopped, plus extra to serve

2 garlic cloves, finely chopped

2 teaspoons dry thyme

¼ teaspoon cayenne pepper

1 pound 2 ounces fresh or thawed, frozen chicken livers, trimmed and halved

3 cups Chicken Stock (see page 168) or store-bought stock

1½ cups easy-cook white rice

salt and freshly ground black pepper

chopped parsley leaves, to serve

hot pepper sauce, to serve

Heat the oil in a large skillet over high heat. Lower the heat to medium, add the celery, peppers and onion and fry, stirring, 2 minutes. Add the scallions, garlic, thyme and cayenne pepper and fry 5 to 7 minutes longer until the onions are soft and starting to turn golden.

Add the chicken livers to the pan, adding extra oil if necessary, and fry until they are brown all over but still pink in the middle.

Add the stock and bring to a boil, then pour the mixture into the slow cooker. Stir in the rice and season with salt and pepper.

Cover the cooker with the lid and cook on HIGH 1½ hours until the chicken livers are cooked through and the rice is tender. Remove the lid and add a little more salt and pepper, if you like.

Switch the cooker off. Put a clean dish towel over the rice, re-cover with the lid and leave to stand at least 5 minutes. The rice mixture can be left covered with the dish towel up to 30 minutes. Just before serving, fluff up the rice with a fork. Sprinkle with parsley and scallions and serve with hot pepper sauce.

CHICKEN KATZU CURRY

PREPARATION TIME: 20 minutes, plus making the stock (optional)
COOKING TIME: 2 hours on HIGH   **SERVES 4**

2 cups thinly sliced carrots

1½ cups peeled and chopped small waxy potatoes

4 boneless, skinless chicken breast halves,
about 6 ounces each

2 tablespoons sunflower oil

1 onion, finely chopped

2 large garlic cloves, chopped

1 tablespoon korma curry powder

1 tablespoon ground ginger

2¼ cups Vegetable Stock (see page 169) or
store-bought stock

2 tablespoons tomato paste

2 tablespoons mango chutney

2 tablespoons cornstarch

salt and freshly ground black pepper

cooked jasmine rice, to serve

2 tablespoons sesame seeds, toasted (see page 170),
to serve

Put the carrots and potatoes in the slow cooker. Season the chicken breast halves with salt and pepper and add to the cooker.

Heat 1 tablespoon of the oil in a large skillet over high heat. Lower the heat to medium, add the onion and fry, stirring, 2 minutes. Add the garlic, curry powder and ginger and stir 1 to 3 minutes longer until the onion is soft.

Add the stock, tomato paste and mango chutney, stirring to dissolve the chutney, then season lightly with salt and pepper. Bring to a boil, stirring, then pour the mixture into the cooker.

Cover the cooker with the lid and cook on HIGH 1½ hours.

Put the cornstarch and 2 tablespoons cold water in a small bowl and stir until smooth, then stir the paste into the cooking liquid. Re-cover the cooker and cook 30 minutes longer until the juices from the chicken run clear when the thickest part of the meat is pierced with the tip of a sharp knife or skewer, the vegetables are tender and the cooking juices are slightly thicker. Remove the chicken from the cooker, wrap in foil and leave to rest at least 5 minutes. Re-cover the cooker and leave the setting on HIGH.

When the chicken has rested, cut into bite-size pieces, then return it to the cooker. Add a little more salt and pepper, if you like. Spoon the curry over the rice, sprinkle with toasted sesame seeds and serve.

ASIAN-STYLE POACHED CHICKEN & BOK CHOY

PREPARATION TIME: 20 minutes, plus making the stock (optional)
COOKING TIME: 4 hours 5 minutes on HIGH   **SERVES 4**

a few cilantro sprigs, with crushed stems, plus extra leaves to serve

2 onions, 1 halved and 1 sliced

1 chicken, about 3 pounds 5 ounces, any fat in the cavity removed

2½ cups Chicken Stock (see page 168) or store-bought stock, boiling, plus extra if needed

½ cup dark soy sauce or mushroom soy sauce, plus extra to taste

4 tablespoons Chinese rice wine

4 garlic cloves, sliced

1-inch piece galangal, sliced

1 dry red Thai chili, seeded if you like

2 scallions, thinly sliced

2 bok choy, quartered

ground Szechuan pepper or freshly ground black pepper

cooked long-grain rice, to serve

Put an upturned heatproof saucer in the slow cooker. (Check that the chicken will be able to sit on top of the saucer with the cooker lid in place.) Heat the covered cooker on HIGH.

Put the cilantro and onion halves in the chicken's cavity and season with pepper. Secure the opening with wooden toothpicks. Put the chicken in the cooker, breast-side down, then pour the stock, soy sauce and rice wine over. Add extra stock to fill the container, if necessary, leaving a 1-inch gap at the top of the pot. The chicken will not be completely covered with liquid. Push the sliced onion, garlic, galangal and chili into the liquid.

Cover the cooker with the lid. Cook on HIGH 3¾ hours until the juices from the chicken run clear when the thickest part of the meat is pierced with the tip of a sharp knife or skewer. Remove the chicken from the cooker, wrap in foil and leave to rest about 10 minutes. Put the scallions and bok choy in the cooker, re-cover and cook 20 minutes longer until the bok choy is tender. Remove the bok choy from the cooker, and wrap in the foil with the chicken.

Pour the cooking liquid into a saucepan and bring to a boil, then boil vigorously at least 3 minutes until it reduces. Add a little more soy sauce and pepper, if you like. Remove the skin from the chicken and carve. Strain the cooking liquid, discarding the solids. Sprinkle the extra cilantro over the chicken and serve with the cooking liquid, bok choy and rice.

CHICKEN TAGINE

PREPARATION TIME: 20 minutes, plus making the stock (optional)
COOKING TIME: 1½ hours on HIGH **SERVES 4**

1 tablespoon olive oil, plus extra if needed

2 pounds chicken thighs, skins removed

½ cup green olives stuffed with pimientos

1 can (15-oz.) chickpeas, drained and rinsed

¾ cup ready-to-eat dry apricots

2 bay leaves, torn

2 preserved lemons, sliced

1 onion, chopped

4 garlic cloves, chopped

2 tablespoons ground coriander

2 tablespoons ground cumin

1 tablespoon ground ginger

½ teaspoon red pepper flakes, or to taste

a large pinch saffron threads

2½ cups Chicken Stock (see page 168), Vegetable Stock (see page 169) or store-bought stock

1½-inch piece gingerroot, or to taste

salt and freshly ground black pepper

chopped cilantro leaves, to serve

cooked couscous, to serve

Heat the oil in a large skillet over high heat. Lower the heat to medium. Add the chicken thighs, skin-side down, and fry 3 to 5 minutes until golden brown, working in batches to avoid overcrowding the pan and adding extra oil, if necessary. Use a slotted spoon to transfer the chicken thighs to the slow cooker as they brown. Add the olives, chickpeas, dry apricots, bay leaves and preserved lemons to the cooker.

Pour off any excess fat from the pan, leaving about 1 tablespoon. Add the onion and fry, stirring, 2 minutes. Add the garlic and spices and fry 1 to 3 minutes longer until the onion is soft.

Add the stock and bring to a boil, scraping the bottom of the pan, then pour the mixture into the cooker and season lightly with salt and pepper. The chicken will not be completely covered with liquid.

Cover the cooker with the lid. Cook on HIGH 1½ hours until the juices from the chicken run clear when the thickest part of the meat is pierced with the tip of a sharp knife or skewer. Use a large metal spoon to skim any excess fat from the surface of the cooking liquid. Remove and discard the bay leaves, then finely grate the unpeeled ginger directly into the pot and add a little more salt and pepper, if you like. Sprinkle with cilantro and serve with couscous.

3.45

CHICKEN WITH TURKISH WALNUT SAUCE

PREPARATION TIME: 20 minutes
COOKING TIME: 3¾ hours on HIGH   **SERVES 4**

2 onions, 1 halved and 1 thinly sliced

1 handful cilantro with crushed stems

1 chicken, about 3 pounds 5 ounces, any fat in the cavity removed

2 bay leaves

1 carrot, thinly sliced

1 celery stick, thinly sliced

1 cinnamon stick

½ teaspoon salt

freshly ground black pepper

chopped dill sprigs, shredded cilantro leaves or chopped parsley leaves, to serve

pomegranate seeds, to serve

green salad, to serve

WALNUT SAUCE

1 cup walnut halves

2 slices day-old bread, crusts removed and torn into pieces

½ cup light cream

a pinch sweet paprika, or to taste

Put an upturned heatproof saucer in the slow cooker. (Check that the chicken will be able to sit on top of the saucer with the cooker lid in place.) Heat the covered cooker on HIGH.

Put the onion halves and cilantro in the chicken's cavity and season with salt and pepper. Secure the opening with wooden toothpicks. Put the chicken in the cooker, breast-side down, then push in the sliced onion, bay leaves, carrot, celery and cinnamon stick. Pour over enough water to fill the container, leaving a 1-inch gap at the top of the pot. Stir in the salt and season with pepper. The chicken will not be completely covered with liquid.

Cover the cooker with the lid. Cook on HIGH 3¾ hours until the juices from the chicken run clear when the thickest part of the meat is pierced.

Meanwhile, make the sauce. Heat a skillet over high heat. Add the walnuts and dry-fry 2 to 3 minutes, shaking the pan occasionally to make sure they do not burn. Transfer ¾ cup of the walnuts to a mini food processor. Add the bread and blitz until finely ground. Chop the remaining walnuts and leave to one side.

Remove the chicken from the cooker, cover and leave to rest 10 minutes. Meanwhile, add the cream, paprika and 2 tablespoons of the cooking liquid to the mini food processor, adding more liquid to form a thick pouring sauce. Season with salt and pepper. Remove the skin from the chicken and carve. Spoon the sauce over the chicken, sprinkle with the chopped walnuts, dill and pomegranate seeds and serve with a green salad.

3.45

FRENCH "ROAST" LEMON & THYME CHICKEN

PREPARATION TIME: 25 minutes, plus making the stock (optional)
COOKING TIME: 3¾ hours on HIGH **SERVES 4**

2 tablespoons butter, soft

8 thyme sprigs

finely grated zest of ½ lemon, with the whole lemon reserved and pricked all over with a fork

1 chicken, about 3 pounds 5 ounces, any fat in the cavity removed

2 garlic cloves, smashed

1 shallot, sliced

2 tablespoons goose fat or duck fat, or 2 tablespoons olive oil

1 celery stick, chopped

1 onion, sliced

1 cup Chicken Stock (see page 168) or store-bought stock

½ cup dry white wine

salt and freshly ground black pepper

sautéed potatoes, to serve

Put an upturned heatproof saucer in the slow cooker. (Check that the chicken will be able to sit on top of the saucer with the cooker lid in place.) Heat the covered cooker on HIGH.

Mix together the butter, leaves from 3 of the thyme sprigs and the lemon zest and season with salt and pepper. Carefully ease your hand under the skin of the chicken, then gently lift the skin, taking care not to tear it. Ease three-quarters of the butter under the skin and rub it over the flesh, then rub the remaining butter over the skin.

Put the remaining thyme in the chicken's cavity with the garlic, shallot and whole lemon and season with salt and pepper. Secure the opening with wooden toothpicks. Season the breasts with salt and pepper.

Melt the goose fat in a skillet over a medium-high heat. Add the chicken and fry, breast-side down, 3 minutes until golden. Put the celery and onion in the cooker, add the chicken and cover with the lid.

Pour off any excess fat from the pan. Add the stock and wine and boil, scraping the bottom, until reduced by about one-third, then pour into the cooker. The chicken will not be completely covered with liquid. Re-cover the cooker and cook on HIGH 3¾ hours until the juices run clear when the thickest part of the meat is pierced. Remove the chicken, cover and leave to rest 5 minutes.

Meanwhile, skim any excess fat from the cooking liquid. Strain the cooking liquid and the juices from the chicken cavity into a saucepan. Boil until reduced by one-third. Spoon the juices over the chicken and serve with sautéed potatoes.

CHICKEN & SMOKED HAM GUMBO

PREPARATION TIME: 35 minutes, plus making the stock (optional)
COOKING TIME: 1½ hours on HIGH   **SERVES 4**

3 tablespoons corn oil

½ cup all-purpose flour

1 large onion, chopped

4 garlic cloves, chopped

1 celery stick, halved lengthwise and chopped

1 green bell pepper, halved lengthwise, seeded and diced

1½ cups Chicken Stock (see page 168), Vegetable Stock (see page 169) or store-bought stock

1 can (15-oz.) crushed tomatoes

4 okra, trimmed and sliced

1 tablespoon dry thyme

1 teaspoon smoked paprika

¼ teaspoon red pepper flakes, or to taste

¾ cup fresh or thawed, frozen corn kernels

2 tablespoons tomato paste

a pinch light brown sugar

14 ounces boneless, skinless chicken thighs, cut into thick strips

10 ounces smoked ham, trimmed and diced

2 bay leaves

4 tablespoons chopped parsley leaves, plus extra to serve

1 teaspoon lemon juice, to taste (optional)

salt and freshly ground black pepper

cooked long-grain rice, to serve

hot pepper sauce, to serve

Heat the oil in a large skillet over high heat. Lower the heat to medium-low, then sprinkle the flour over and stir to make a thick paste. Continue stirring 15 to 20 minutes until the paste turns a hazelnut color. It will be very slow to change color, then change quickly, so watch closely so it does not burn.

Add the onion, garlic, celery and pepper and stir 3 to 5 minutes longer until the onion is soft.

Add the stock, crushed tomatoes, okra, thyme, paprika, red pepper flakes, corn, tomato paste and brown sugar and bring to a boil, stirring, then pour the mixture into the slow cooker. Stir in the chicken, ham and bay leaves and season with salt and pepper.

Cover the cooker with the lid. Cook on HIGH 1½ hours until the juices from the chicken run clear when the thickest part of the meat is pierced with the tip of a sharp knife or skewer. Remove and discard the bay leaves. Stir in the parsley and lemon juice, if using, and add a little more salt and pepper, if you like. Spoon the gumbo over the rice, sprinkle with parsley and serve with hot pepper sauce.

COOK'S TIP
If you need to thaw frozen corn kernels in a hurry, put them in a strainer and rinse under hot running water. Alternatively, soak the kernels in a bowl of boiling water 3 minutes, then drain well.

GLAZED DRUMSTICKS

PREPARATION TIME: 10 minutes, plus
   up to 24 hours marinating
COOKING TIME: 2 hours on HIGH   **SERVES 4**

⅔ cup soy sauce
2 tablespoons rice wine vinegar
5 tablespoons dark brown sugar
4 large garlic cloves, smashed
1 tablespoon ground coriander
1 tablespoon ground cumin
4 scallions, finely chopped, plus extra to serve
1 handful cilantro leaves, finely chopped
8 chicken drumsticks, skinned
2 tablespoons arrowroot or cornstarch
7 ounces snow peas, trimmed
freshly ground black pepper
cooked rice or noodles, to serve

Put the soy sauce, vinegar, brown sugar, garlic, coriander, cumin, scallions and cilantro in a large nonmetallic bowl and stir until the sugar dissolves. Add the drumsticks, then rub the mixture all over them. Season with pepper. Cover and marinate in the refrigerator up to 24 hours.

Transfer the drumsticks and all of the marinade to the slow cooker. The drumsticks will not be completely covered with liquid.

Cover the cooker with the lid and cook on HIGH 1½ hours, turning once after 1 hour. Put the arrowroot and 2 tablespoons cold water in a bowl and stir until smooth, then stir the paste into the cooking liquid. Re-cover the cooker and cook 15 minutes. Add the snow peas, re-cover and cook 15 minutes until the juices from the chicken run clear when the thickest part of the meat is pierced. Sprinkle with scallions and serve with rice.

TURKEY & RED CABBAGE

PREPARATION TIME: 10 minutes
COOKING TIME: 4 hours on HIGH   **SERVES 4**

1 tablespoon smoked or sweet paprika, or to taste
1½ pounds boneless, skinless turkey breast half
1 can (15-oz.) cannellini beans, drained and rinsed
2 bay leaves, torn
1 tablespoon dry tarragon or parsley
turkey bones (optional)
2 cups apple juice, plus extra if needed
2 cups cored and thinly sliced red cabbage
1 long strip lemon peel, pith removed
salt and freshly ground black pepper
chopped parsley leaves, to serve

Rub the paprika all over the turkey breast, then put it in the slow cooker. Add the beans to the cooker, tucking them down around the turkey. Add the bay leaves, tarragon and turkey bones, if using.

Pour the apple juice over, making sure the beans are covered. The turkey breast might not be covered with liquid. Season with salt and pepper.

Cover the cooker with the lid. Cook on HIGH 3½ hours until the juices from the turkey run clear when the thickest part of the meat is pierced with the tip of a sharp knife or skewer. Remove the turkey from the cooker, wrap in foil and leave to rest about 10 minutes.

Skim any excess fat from the cooking liquid. Add the cabbage and lemon peel. Re-cover the cooker and cook 30 minutes until the cabbage is tender. Remove and discard the bay leaves and lemon peel, then slice the turkey. Add the beans and cabbage and spoon the cooking liquid over. Sprinkle with parsley and serve.

TURKEY, SWEET POTATO & CORN CHILI

This is a good one-pot dinner for when you want a simple meal. Its depth of flavor comes from the ancho chili powder, but if you can't find any, use 2 tablespoons chili con carne seasoning and omit the ground cumin from the ingredients.

PREPARATION TIME: 15 minutes, plus making the tortilla chips (optional)
COOKING TIME: 2¼ hours on HIGH   **SERVES 4**

4 tablespoons tomato paste

2 tablespoons sunflower oil

1 onion, finely chopped

2 large garlic cloves, crushed

1 tablespoon ancho chili powder, or to taste

1½ teaspoons ground cumin

a pinch cayenne pepper (optional)

1 pound 2 ounces lean ground turkey

1 can (15-oz.) crushed tomatoes

1½ cups finely diced sweet potato

½ can (15-oz.) canned pinto beans, drained and rinsed

½ can (15-oz.) canned corn kernels, drained and rinsed

1 bay leaf

salt and freshly ground black pepper

cooked white rice, to serve

chopped cilantro or parsley leaves, to serve

1 recipe quantity Tortilla Chips (see page 174) or corn chips, to serve (optional)

Put the tomato paste and 4 tablespoons water in a small bowl and stir until it dissolves, then leave to one side.

Heat 1 tablespoon of the oil in a large skillet over high heat. Lower the heat to medium, add the onion and fry, stirring, 2 minutes. Add the garlic, chili powder, cumin and cayenne pepper, if using, and stir 1 to 3 minutes longer until the onion is soft. Use a slotted spoon to transfer the mixture to the slow cooker.

Heat the remaining oil in the pan. Add the turkey and fry 2 to 3 minutes, breaking up the meat, until brown all over. Use a slotted spoon to transfer the turkey to the cooker, leaving behind as much oil as possible. Add the tomato paste mixture and all the remaining ingredients to the cooker and stir. Season with salt and pepper.

Cover the cooker with the lid. Cook on HIGH 2¼ hours, stirring once halfway through, until the turkey is tender and the flavors are blended. Remove and discard the bay leaf and add a little more salt and pepper, if you like. Spoon the chili over the rice, sprinkle with cilantro and serve with Tortilla Chips, if you like.

DUCK TAGINE

PREPARATION TIME: 20 minutes
COOKING TIME: 1½ hours on HIGH **SERVES 4**

4 duck legs, about 9 ounces each, skin scored

3 ounces fresh chorizo, skinned and sliced

1 zucchini, halved lengthwise and thinly sliced

1 tablespoon olive oil, if needed

1 onion, thinly sliced

2 garlic cloves, finely chopped

1 tablespoon fennel seeds

1 tablespoon dry thyme

2 teaspoons ground coriander

a pinch red pepper flakes, or to taste

½ cup dry white wine

1 can (15-oz.) crushed tomatoes

2 long strips orange peel, pith removed

12 pitted prunes

2 tablespoons freshly squeezed orange juice, or to taste (optional)

salt and freshly ground black pepper

chopped cilantro leaves, to serve

pine nuts, toasted (see page 170), to serve

cooked couscous, to serve

Heat a skillet over high heat. Add the duck legs, skin-side down, and fry 3 to 5 minutes until the fat under the skin melts into the pan. Use a slotted spoon to transfer the duck legs to the slow cooker as they brown.

Pour off any excess fat from the pan, leaving about 1 tablespoon. Lower the heat to medium, add the chorizo and fry, stirring, 1 to 2 minutes until it gives off its fat and starts to crisp. Use a slotted spoon to transfer the chorizo to the cooker, then add the zucchini to the cooker.

If there is less than 1 tablespoon of fat remaining in the pan, add the oil and heat. When the oil is hot, add the onion and fry, stirring, 2 minutes. Add the garlic, fennel seeds, thyme, coriander and red pepper flakes and fry 1 to 3 minutes longer until the onion is soft. Pour the wine over, bring to a boil and boil until it almost evaporates. Add the crushed tomatoes and orange peel and season with salt and pepper. Bring to a boil, scraping the bottom of the pan, then pour the mixture into the cooker. The ingredients in the cooker will not be completely covered with liquid. Add the prunes, tucking them down among the duck legs.

Cover the cooker with the lid. Cook on HIGH 1½ hours until the juices from the duck run clear when the thickest part of the meat is pierced with the tip of a sharp knife or skewer. Remove and discard the orange peel. Season with a little more salt and pepper, if you like, and stir in the orange juice, if using. Sprinkle with cilantro and toasted pine nuts and serve with couscous.

VIETNAMESE CARAMEL PORK & CARROTS

Heating sugar and water to make caramel isn't difficult but it does take practice to heat the syrup until it is dark enough to have a rich, deep flavor without burning it. To gauge the color accurately, use a stainless-steel pan, rather than a dark one. Take care when you stop the caramel cooking, because the sauce will splutter.

PREPARATION TIME: 20 minutes, plus pickling the bean sprouts (optional)
COOKING TIME: 8¼ hours on LOW   **SERVES 4**

2 cups thinly sliced carrots

2 red Thai shallots or 1 French shallot, halved lengthwise and sliced

1 lemongrass stalk, outer layer removed, bruised and cut in half

1 pound 10 ounces boneless pork leg, trimmed of fat and cut into large chunks

chopped salted peanuts, to serve

cilantro leaves, to serve

cooked jasmine rice, to serve

1 recipe quantity Pickled Bean Sprouts (see page 173), to serve (optional)

VIETNAMESE CARAMEL SAUCE

¾ cup soft light brown sugar

1 tablespoon fish sauce, plus extra to taste

1½ teaspoons lime juice, plus extra to taste

To make the caramel sauce, put the sugar and 2 tablespoons water in a saucepan over medium heat and stir until the sugar dissolves. Increase the heat to high and boil, without stirring, until the caramel turns a dark golden brown color. Watch closely because it can burn quickly. Immediately remove the pan from the heat and add the fish sauce and lime juice to stop the cooking process.

Put the carrots, shallots and lemongrass in the slow cooker. Add the pork and pour the caramel sauce over.

Cover the cooker with the lid and cook on LOW 4 hours, then stir through to prevent the pork and carrots sticking together. Re-cover the cooker as quickly as possible and cook 4¼ hours longer until the pork is tender. Remove the pork and carrots from the cooker, wrap in foil and keep warm.

Strain the cooking liquid into a small saucepan, discarding the solids, and bring to a boil over high heat. Boil 3 minutes until the cooking liquid reduces to about ½ cup. Add a little more fish sauce and lime juice, if you like. Stir in the pork and carrots and toss well to coat. Sprinkle with peanuts and cilantro and serve with rice and Pickled Bean Sprouts, if you like.

9

SOUTHERN "BAKED" BEANS WITH SMOKED HAM

PREPARATION TIME: 20 minutes, plus making the stock (optional)
COOKING TIME: 1 hour on HIGH, plus 8 hours on LOW   **SERVES 4**

1 bone-in smoked ham hock, about 3 pounds 2 ounces

4 tablespoons Vegetable Stock (see page 169), store-bought stock or water

1 can (15-oz.) crushed tomatoes

⅔ cup soft light brown sugar

2 bay leaves, torn

2 large garlic cloves, finely chopped

1 onion, finely chopped

1 tablespoon dry thyme

2 teaspoons ground cumin

½ teaspoon red pepper flakes, or to taste

2 cans (15-oz.) borlotti beans or pinto beans, drained and rinsed

salt and freshly ground black pepper

chopped parsley leaves, to serve

cornbread or cooked American long-grain rice, to serve (optional)

Put the ham hock in a large saucepan and cover with water. Cover with a lid and bring to a boil over high heat.

Meanwhile, put the stock, crushed tomatoes, brown sugar, bay leaves, garlic, onion, thyme, cumin and red pepper flakes in the slow cooker, stirring to dissolve the sugar. Season with salt and pepper, remembering the ham might still be salty.

When the ham water boils, transfer the ham hock to a large colander and rinse well. Transfer the hock to the slow cooker.

Add the beans to the cooker, tucking them down around the hock. The ham and all the beans might not be completely covered with liquid.

Cover the cooker with the lid and cook on HIGH 1 hour, then switch the cooker to LOW and cook 8 hours longer until the gammon is tender and the meat is falling off the bone. Remove the hock from the cooker and leave to cool slightly. Remove and discard the bay leaves. Re-cover the cooker to keep the beans warm.

When the ham hock is cool enough to handle, remove all the meat from the bone, discarding the fat, gristle and skin. Cut the meat into portions, then return to the cooker to heat through, if necessary. Season with salt and a little more pepper, if you like. Sprinkle with parsley and serve with cornbread, if you like.

(5)

COWBOY PORK & BEANS

PREPARATION TIME: 25 minutes, plus making the stock (optional)
COOKING TIME: 5 hours on HIGH   **SERVES 4**

1 tablespoon sunflower oil

1½ pounds pork belly, cut into strips along the grain, then cut into bite-size pieces

1 can (15-oz.) red kidney beans, drained and rinsed

1 can (15-oz.) black beans, drained and rinsed

1 onion, finely chopped

2 garlic cloves, finely chopped

1 tablespoon ground coriander

1 tablespoon ground cumin

1 tablespoon dry thyme or dry oregano

½ teaspoon cayenne pepper, or to taste

1 can (15-oz.) crushed tomatoes

1 cup Vegetable Stock (see page 169), Beef Stock (see page 168) or store-bought stock, plus extra if needed

2 cups thinly sliced carrots

2 tablespoons tomato paste

2 tablespoons molasses or dark brown sugar

1 teaspoon Worcestershire sauce, or to taste

salt and freshly ground black pepper

chopped parsley leaves, to serve

cooked long-grain rice, to serve

Heat the oil in a large skillet over high heat. Add the pork and fry 3 to 5 minutes until brown on all sides and as much fat as possible melts into the pan, working in batches, if necessary. Watch closely, making sure the edges do not burn. Transfer the pork to the slow cooker as it browns, then add all the beans.

Pour off any excess fat from the pan, leaving about 1 tablespoon. Add the onion and fry, stirring, 2 minutes. Add the garlic, coriander, cumin, thyme and cayenne pepper and fry 1 to 3 minutes longer until the onion is soft.

Add the crushed tomatoes, stock, carrots, tomato paste and molasses and season with salt and pepper. Bring to a boil, stirring, then pour the mixture into the cooker. There should be enough liquid to cover the pork and beans, but do not worry if they are not completely submerged.

Cover the cooker and cook on HIGH 5 hours until the pork is tender. Stir in the Worcestershire sauce and add a little more pepper, if you like. Sprinkle with parsley and serve with rice.

ITALIAN PORK STEW WITH SUMMER HERBS

Don't be alarmed by the quantity of dry herbs in this recipe—it isn't a typing error. After the stew simmers for eight hours, the herbs mellow and the flavor of mint shines through. I find this dish particularly welcome in the middle of winter, when dry herbs really come into their own.

PREPARATION TIME: 25 minutes, plus making the stock (optional)
COOKING TIME: 8 hours on LOW   **SERVES 4**

1½ pounds boneless pork shoulder, trimmed of fat and cut into large chunks

1 can (15-oz.) chickpeas, drained and rinsed

1 can (15-oz.) plum tomatoes

2 tablespoons olive oil

1 onion, finely chopped

1 carrot, finely chopped

1 celery stick, finely chopped

4 garlic cloves, finely chopped

1 cup tomato paste

½ cup Vegetable Stock (see page 169) or store-bought stock, plus extra if needed

2 to 3 tablespoons dry mint

1 tablespoon dry thyme

1 tablespoon dry oregano

a pinch sugar

salt and freshly ground black pepper

finely shredded mint or chopped parsley leaves, to serve

soft polenta, to serve

Put the pork, chickpeas and plum tomatoes in the slow cooker.

Heat the oil in a large skillet over high heat. Lower the heat to medium, add the onion, carrot and celery and fry, stirring, 2 minutes. Add the garlic and fry 1 to 3 minutes longer until the onion is soft.

Add the tomato paste, stock, dry herbs and sugar, then season with salt and pepper and bring to a boil. Boil, stirring, 3 minutes until the liquid reduces by about one-third, then pour the mixture into the cooker. Stir well and add extra stock, if necessary, to just cover the chickpeas.

Cover the cooker with the lid and cook on LOW 8 hours until the pork is tender. Add a little more salt and pepper, if you like. Sprinkle with mint and serve with soft polenta.

PORK PAPRIKASH

PREPARATION TIME: 30 minutes
COOKING TIME: 8 hours on LOW, plus 30 minutes on HIGH   **SERVES 4**

1½ pounds boneless pork shoulder, trimmed of fat and cut into large chunks

2 tablespoons sunflower oil, plus extra if needed

1 large onion, finely chopped

1½ pounds cremini mushrooms, sliced

1 tablespoon smoked paprika

1 tablespoon dry dill

1 tablespoon cornstarch

1 cup condensed cream of mushroom soup

2 green bell peppers, halved lengthwise, seeded and diced

4 tablespoons sour cream

10 ounces dry tagliatelle or other flat noodles

2 tablespoons butter

salt and freshly ground black pepper

chopped parsley leaves or chopped dill, to serve

Season the pork with salt and pepper. Heat the oil in a large skillet over high heat. Lower the heat to medium, add the pork and fry 3 to 5 minutes until brown on all sides, working in batches to avoid overcrowding the pan, and adding extra oil, if necessary. Use a slotted spoon to transfer the pork to the slow cooker as it browns.

Add the onion to the skillet and fry, stirring, 3 to 5 minutes until soft. Add the mushrooms, sprinkle with salt and fry 5 to 8 minutes until all the liquid is absorbed, working in batches, if necessary. Sprinkle the paprika and dill over the mushrooms and stir 30 seconds.

Put the cornstarch and 2 tablespoons cold water in a small bowl and stir until smooth. Add the cornstarch paste and mushroom soup to the pan and bring to a boil, scraping the bottom of the pan. Pour the mixture into the cooker and stir well. Season lightly with salt and pepper.

Cover the cooker with the lid and cook on LOW 8 hours. Stir in the peppers and sour cream. Switch the cooker to HIGH, re-cover and cook 30 minutes until the pork and peppers are tender.

Twenty minutes before serving, bring a large saucepan of salted water to the boil. Add the tagliatelle and cook 10 minutes, or according to the package directions, until tender. Drain well, shaking off any excess water, then return the noodles to the hot pan. Add the butter and stir until it melts. Spoon the paprikash over the tagliatelle and season with a little more salt and pepper, if you like. Sprinkle with parsley and serve.

HAM WITH EGG & PARSLEY SAUCE

PREPARATION TIME: 20 minutes, plus making the stock (optional) and sauce
COOKING TIME: 9½ hours on LOW, plus 30 minutes on HIGH   **SERVES 4**

1 unsmoked ham knuckle, about 3¼ pounds

3 cups Vegetable Stock (see page 169) or store-bought stock, plus extra if needed

4 cloves

2 bay leaves, torn

4 cups cored and sliced white cabbage

salt and freshly ground black pepper

1 recipe quantity Egg & Parsley Sauce (see page 172), to serve

boiled small waxy potatoes, to serve

Put the ham knuckle in a large saucepan and cover with water. Cover with a lid and bring to a boil over high heat. When the ham water boils, transfer the knuckle to a large colander and drain and rinse well. Transfer the ham to the slow cooker. Add the stock, cloves and bay leaves, adding extra stock to cover the ham, if necessary. Season with pepper.

Cover the cooker with the lid and cook on LOW 9½ hours. Use a large metal spoon to skim any excess fat from the surface of the cooking liquid. Remove and discard the cloves and bay leaves. Season with salt and a little more pepper, if you like, remembering the ham might have made the cooking liquid salty. Stir in the cabbage.

Switch the cooker to HIGH, re-cover and cook 30 minutes until the ham and cabbage are tender. Remove the knuckle from the cooker and leave to cool slightly. Re-cover the cooker to keep the cabbage warm.

When the ham is cool enough to handle, remove all the meat from the bone, discarding the fat, gristle and skin. Cut the meat into portions, then remove the cabbage from the cooker, using a slotted spoon, and shake off any excess liquid. Serve the ham and cabbage with Egg & Parsley Sauce and with small waxy potatoes.

CHORIZO & BLACK BEAN RICE

I developed this version of the Spanish festival dish *Moros y Christianos*,
for a quick-and-easy midweek dinner. The chorizo adds piquancy and extra protein.
For a vegetarian version, omit the chorizo and fry the onion with the garlic, chili and
spices listed, then add 1 teaspoon smoked paprika and cayenne pepper.

PREPARATION TIME: 20 minutes, plus making the stock (optional) and at least 5 minutes standing
COOKING TIME: 1½ hours on HIGH   **SERVES 4**

1 tablespoon olive oil

2½ ounces fresh chorizo, skinned and diced

1 large onion, finely chopped

4 large garlic cloves, finely chopped

1 green chili, seeded if you like, and thinly sliced

1 tablespoon dry dill

1 teaspoon ground cumin

3 cups Vegetable Stock (see page 169)
or store-bought stock

1 can (15-oz.) black beans, drained and rinsed

1½ cups easy-cook white rice

2 sun-dry tomatoes in oil, drained and thinly sliced

2 tablespoons finely chopped parsley leaves

salt and freshly ground black pepper

Heat the oil in a large skillet over high heat. Lower the heat to medium, add the chorizo and fry, stirring, 1 to 2 minutes until it gives off its fat and starts to crisp. Use a slotted spoon to transfer the chorizo to the slow cooker.

Pour off any excess fat from the pan, leaving about 1 tablespoon. Add the onion and fry, stirring, 2 minutes. Add the garlic, chili, dill and cumin and fry 1 to 3 minutes longer until the onion is soft.

Add the stock and bring to a boil, stirring, then pour the mixture into the cooker. Stir in the beans, rice and sun-dry tomatoes and season with salt and pepper.

Cover the cooker with the lid and cook on HIGH 1½ hours until the rice is tender. Stir in the parsley and add a little more salt and pepper, if you like.

Switch the cooker off. Put a clean dish towel over the rice, re-cover with the lid and leave to stand at least 5 minutes. The rice can be left covered with the dish towel up to 30 minutes. Just before serving, fluff up the rice with a fork. Serve hot.

PULLED PORK

PREPARATION TIME: 10 minutes
COOKING TIME: 12 hours on LOW   **SERVES 4**

2 tablespoons soft light brown sugar
1 teaspoon sweet paprika
2 teaspoons dry rosemary or thyme
½ teaspoon ground ginger
finely grated zest of 1 large lemon
2¼ pounds boneless pork shoulder, with the skin and
    outer layer of fat removed, ideally in one piece
2 onions, sliced
¾ cup dry white wine
salt and freshly ground black pepper
mashed potatoes, to serve

Combine the brown sugar, paprika, rosemary,
ginger and lemon zest in a bowl, then season with
salt and pepper. Rub the mixture all over the pork.
Put the pork, onions and wine in the slow cooker.

Cover the cooker with the lid and cook on LOW
12 hours until the pork is very tender and falling
apart. Gently remove the pork from the cooker,
wrap tightly in foil and leave to rest 10 minutes.

Meanwhile, skim any excess fat from the cooking
liquid. Add a little more salt and pepper, if you
like. Re-cover the cooker with the lid to keep the
cooking liquid warm.

Unwrap the pork, transfer to a rimmed plate to
catch any juices. Use two forks to pull apart and
shred the meat. Pour any remaining juices into the
cooking liquid. Spoon the cooking liquid over the
pork and serve with mashed potatoes.

PORK & SAUERKRAUT

PREPARATION TIME: 12 minutes, plus making
    the applesauce (optional)
COOKING TIME: 2½ hours on HIGH   **SERVES 4**

3½ cups sauerkraut, drained
¾ cup Applesauce (see page 33)
    or store-bought applesauce
1 large carrot, coarsely grated
2 to 4 tablespoons soft brown sugar, to taste
2 tablespoons orange juice
1 teaspoon smoked or sweet paprika, or to taste
4 boneless pork shoulder chops, about 5 ounces each
    and 1 inch thick
2 cups peeled and thinly sliced small waxy potatoes
salt and freshly ground black pepper
chopped parsley leaves, to serve

Mix together the sauerkraut, applesauce, carrot,
brown sugar, orange juice and paprika in a bowl.
Season with salt and pepper and leave to one
side. Season both sides of the pork chops with
salt and pepper.

Arrange the potatoes in a single layer, if possible,
on the bottom of the slow cooker container. Add
half of the sauerkraut mixture, then add the
chops in a single layer and top with the remaining
sauerkraut mixture.

Cover the cooker with the lid and cook on HIGH
2½ hours until the pork is tender when pierced with
the tip of a sharp knife or skewer. Add a little more
salt and pepper, if you like. Sprinkle with parsley
and serve.

5

CHINESE PORK BELLY

This recipe produces a sweet-and-savory cooking juice, ideal for serving with rice.

PREPARATION TIME: 20 minutes, plus 1 hour marinating
COOKING TIME: 5 hours on HIGH   **SERVES 4**

2 tablespoons oyster sauce

2 tablespoons soy sauce, or to taste

4 teaspoons sweet soy sauce, or to taste

2 teaspoons sweet chili sauce

1½ pounds pork belly, cut into strips along the grain,
then cut into bite-size pieces

2 tablespoons garlic-flavored sunflower oil

2 tablespoons honey

1-inch piece galangal, peeled and sliced

4 large garlic cloves, smashed

freshly ground black pepper

sesame oil, to serve

sesame seeds, toasted (see page 170), to serve

chopped cilantro leaves, to serve

cooked short-grain white rice, to serve

Mix together 1 tablespoon of the oyster sauce, 1 tablespoon of the soy sauce, 2 teaspoons of the sweet soy sauce and 1 teaspoon of the chili sauce in a bowl. Add the pork, then use your hands to rub the marinade all over the meat. Cover and leave to marinate 1 hour at room temperature.

Remove the pork from the marinade and reserve the marinade. Pat the pork dry with paper towels. Heat the oil in a large skillet over high heat. Add the pork and fry 3 to 5 minutes until brown on all sides and as much fat as possible melts into the pan, working in batches, if necessary. Watch closely so the edges do not burn. Transfer the pork to the slow cooker as it browns.

Discard the fat in the pan, then wipe the bottom of the pan with paper towels. Add the remaining oyster sauce, soy sauce, sweet soy sauce and chili sauce, honey, galangal, garlic, reserved marinade and ½ cup water and bring to a boil, stirring to dissolve the honey. Season with pepper, then pour over the pork.

Cover the cooker with the lid and cook on HIGH 5 hours until the pork is tender. Add a little more pepper or soy sauce, if you like. Transfer the pork to a bowl, using a slotted spoon. Skim any excess fat from the cooking liquid. Remove and discard the galangal and garlic. Spoon the cooking liquid over the pork. Drizzle with sesame oil, sprinkle with toasted sesame seeds and cilantro and serve with rice.

(4)

SAUSAGE HOTPOT

This is a regular busy-day meal in my house. Not only is it fantastically easy, the variations are endless. You can use whatever canned legumes you have, and it's a great way to use up just about any vegetable—I particularly like to add chopped butternut squash. Spicy sausages work really well, too. And, if I'm in a real hurry, I just skip frying the sausages, onions and peppers.

PREPARATION TIME: 20 minutes, plus making the stock (optional)
COOKING TIME: 4 hours on LOW   **SERVES 4**

1 tablespoon olive oil

8 good-quality link sausages, such as pork and fennel, pricked with a fork

1 large onion, finely chopped

2 large garlic cloves, crushed

1 green bell pepper, halved lengthwise, seeded and thickly sliced

1 red bell pepper, halved lengthwise, seeded and thickly sliced

1 can (15-oz.) legume, such as borlotti beans, cannellini beans, chickpeas, fava beans or red kidney beans, drained and rinsed

1 can (15-oz.) crushed tomatoes with herbs

¼ cup Beef Stock (see page 168), Vegetable Stock (see page 169) or store-bought stock

2 bay leaves

Worcestershire sauce

freshly ground black pepper

chopped parsley leaves, to serve

Dijon, wholegrain or German sweet mustard, to serve

Heat a large skillet over high heat. Lower the heat to medium, add the oil and sausages and fry 3 to 5 minutes until brown all over, working in batches to avoid overcrowding the pan, if necessary. Use a slotted spoon to transfer the sausages to the slow cooker as they brown.

Pour off any excess oil from the pan, leaving about 1 tablespoon. Add the onion and fry, stirring, 2 minutes. Add the garlic and peppers and fry 1 to 3 minutes longer until the onion is soft. Use a slotted spoon to transfer the vegetables to the cooker.

Stir in the legume, crushed tomatoes, stock and bay leaves and season with Worcestershire sauce and pepper. The ingredients will not be completely covered with liquid.

Cover the cooker with the lid. Cook on LOW 4 hours until the sausages are cooked through and the peppers are tender. Remove and discard the bay leaves and add a little more Worcestershire sauce and pepper, if you like. Sprinkle with parsley and serve with some mustard.

6

ROGAN JOSH

PREPARATION TIME: 30 minutes, plus making the raita (optional)
COOKING TIME: 6 hours on LOW   **SERVES 4**

2 garlic cloves, coarsely chopped

1½-inch piece gingerroot, peeled and coarsely chopped

3 tablespoons ghee, peanut oil or sunflower oil, plus extra if needed

1½ pounds boneless lamb shoulder, trimmed of fat and cut into large chunks

2 onions, finely chopped

5 green cardamom pods, lightly crushed

4 cloves

2 cinnamon sticks

2 teaspoons ground cumin

1 teaspoon ground coriander

1 teaspoon sweet paprika

½ teaspoon Kashmiri chili powder or cayenne pepper, or to taste

4 tablespoons tomato paste

2 bay leaves

½ cup plain yogurt

½ teaspoon garam masala

salt and freshly ground black pepper

cilantro leaves, to serve

cooked basmati rice, to serve

1 recipe quantity Cucumber & Tomato Raita (see page 172), to serve (optional)

Put the garlic and ginger in a mini food processor and process until a coarse paste forms, scraping down the side of the bowl as necessary. Leave to one side.

Melt 2 tablespoons of the ghee in a large skillet over high heat. Lower the heat to medium, add the lamb and fry 3 to 5 minutes until brown on all sides, working in batches to avoid overcrowding the pan and adding extra ghee to the pan, if necessary. Use a slotted spoon to transfer the lamb to the slow cooker.

Melt the remaining ghee in the pan. Add the onions and fry, stirring, 2 minutes. Add the garlic and ginger paste and fry 1 to 3 minutes longer until the onion is soft.

Add the spices and cook, stirring, 1 minute until fragrant. Stir in the tomato paste and bay leaves and season with salt and pepper. Add the mixture to the cooker and stir in 2 tablespoons water. Stir well, making sure the lamb is completely coated in the mixture.

Cover the cooker with the lid and cook on LOW 5½ hours until the lamb is tender. Stir well, then mix together the yogurt and 2 tablespoons of the cooking liquid in a bowl. Stir the yogurt mixture into the curry and sprinkle in the garam masala. Re-cover the cooker and cook 30 minutes longer. Remove and discard the bay leaves and cinnamon sticks and add a little more salt and pepper, if you like. Sprinkle with cilantro and serve with rice and Cucumber and Tomato Raita, if you like.

MIDDLE EASTERN LAMB WITH FIGS & HONEY

PREPARATION TIME: 20 minutes
COOKING TIME: 6 hours on LOW, plus 15 minutes on HIGH   **SERVES 4**

2 tablespoons olive oil, plus extra if needed

1 fennel bulb, sliced

2 garlic cloves, chopped

1 tablespoon ground coriander

2 teaspoons ground cumin

½ teaspoon ground cloves

a pinch red pepper flakes, or to taste (optional)

1½ pounds boneless lamb shoulder, trimmed of fat and cut into large chunks

½ cup dry figs, coarsely chopped

2 preserved lemons, sliced

1 tablespoon honey

lamb bones (optional; you can ask a butcher for these)

4 fresh figs, quartered

1 to 2 tablespoons lemon or lime juice (optional)

salt and freshly ground black pepper

chopped cilantro leaves, to serve

finely grated lemon or lime zest, to serve

2 tablespoons sesame seeds, toasted (see page 170), to serve

flatbread, to serve (optional)

Heat 1 tablespoon of the oil in a large skillet over high heat. Lower the heat to medium, add the fennel and fry, stirring, 2 minutes. Add the garlic and spices and fry 2 minutes longer. Transfer the mixture to the slow cooker, then wipe the pan with paper towels.

Heat the remaining oil in the pan. Add the lamb and fry 3 to 5 minutes until brown on all sides, working in batches to avoid overcrowding the pan and adding extra oil, if necessary. Use a slotted spoon to transfer the lamb to the cooker.

Add the dry figs, preserved lemons, honey and lamb bones, if using, to the cooker. Pour ¾ cup boiling water over, stirring to dissolve the honey, then season with salt and pepper.

Cover the cooker with the lid and cook on LOW 6 hours until the lamb is tender. Remove the lamb from the cooker, using a slotted spoon, then wrap in foil and leave to rest about 10 minutes. Remove and discard the preserved lemons and lamb bones, if necessary. Skim any excess fat from the cooking liquid, then add the fresh figs. Switch the cooker to HIGH, re-cover and cook 15 minutes until the figs are tender but still retain their shape.

Return the lamb and any cooking juices to the cooker and gently stir into the sauce. Add a little more salt and pepper and the lemon juice, if you like. Sprinkle cilantro, lemon zest and toasted sesame seeds over the lamb and figs and serve with flatbread, if you like.

FRENCH LAMB & FLAGEOLET BEANS

PREPARATION: 20 minutes, plus making the stock (optional)
COOKING TIME: 8¼ hours on LOW   **SERVES 4**

2 large garlic cloves, peeled

2 pounds boneless lamb shoulder, rolled and tied

4 rosemary sprigs

2 tablespoons garlic-flavored olive oil

2 shallots, finely chopped

2 cups full-bodied dry red wine

1 cup Vegetable Stock (see page 169) or store-bought stock, plus extra if needed

2 bay leaves

2 cans (15-oz.) flageolet beans, drained and rinsed

salt and freshly ground black pepper

sautéed potatoes, to serve

Put the garlic on a cutting board, lightly sprinkle with salt and use the tip of a knife to crush into a paste. Using a small, sharp knife, make thin, deep slits all over the lamb, then use your fingers to push the garlic paste into the slits. Push one of the rosemary sprigs and any remaining garlic paste into the middle of the rolled lamb.

Heat the oil in a large skillet over high heat. Lower the heat to medium, add the lamb and fry 5 to 8 minutes until brown all over. Transfer the lamb to the slow cooker.

Pour off any excess fat from the pan, leaving about 1 tablespoon. Add the shallots and fry, stirring, 2 to 3 minutes until golden. Add the wine, stock, bay leaves and remaining rosemary sprigs and season with salt and pepper. Bring to a boil, scraping the bottom of the pan, and boil until the liquid reduces by one-third. Pour the mixture into the cooker. The lamb will not be completely covered with liquid.

Cover the cooker with the lid and cook on LOW 6 hours. Turn the lamb over, using tongs. Add the beans and stir well. The beans will not be completely covered with liquid. Re-cover the cooker as quickly as possible and cook 2¼ hours longer until the lamb is cooked through and tender.

Remove the lamb, wrap in foil and leave to rest 10 minutes. Remove and discard the rosemary and bay leaves, and season with a little more salt and pepper, if you like. Re-cover the cooker to keep the beans warm. When the lamb has rested, carve the meat and serve with the beans and cooking juices, and with sautéed potatoes.

10

TUSCAN LAMB SHANKS & BUTTER BEANS

PREPARATION TIME: 30 minutes, plus making the stock (optional)
COOKING TIME: 10 hours on LOW   **SERVES 4**

4 lamb shanks, about 14 ounces each

2 tablespoons olive oil, plus extra if needed

2 carrots, finely chopped

1 celery stick, finely chopped

1 onion, finely chopped

6 large garlic cloves, finely chopped

3 cups dry red or white wine

1 cup Beef Stock (see page 168), Vegetable Stock (see page 169) or store-bought stock, plus extra if needed

2 bay leaves

leaves from 3 rosemary stems and 1 tablespoon dry sage, tied in a piece of cheesecloth, plus extra chopped rosemary leaves, to serve

1 can (15-oz.) butter or fava beans, drained and rinsed

1 teaspoon balsamic vinegar, plus extra to taste

salt and freshly ground black pepper

Season the lamb shanks with salt and pepper. Heat the oil in a large skillet over high heat. Lower the heat to medium, add the lamb shanks and fry 5 to 8 minutes until brown on both sides, working in batches to avoid overcrowding the pan and adding extra oil to the pan, if necessary. Use tongs to transfer the lamb shanks to the slow cooker as they brown.

Pour off any excess fat from the pan, leaving about 1 tablespoon. Add the carrots, celery and onion and fry, stirring, 2 minutes. Add the garlic and fry 1 to 3 minutes longer until the onion is soft.

Add the wine, stock, bay leaves and herb bundle and season with salt and pepper. Bring to a boil, scraping the bottom of the pan, and boil until the liquid reduces by half. Pour the mixture into the cooker. The lamb shanks will not be completely covered with liquid. Push the bay leaves and herb bundle down among the shanks.

Cover the cooker with the lid and cook on LOW 6 hours. Remove the lamb shanks from the cooker, then stir the beans into the cooking liquid. Return the meat to the cooker, adding the shanks that were previously near the top of the cooker first. Re-cover the cooker as quickly as possible and cook 4 hours longer until the lamb is tender and the beans are hot.

Remove and discard the bay leaves and herb bundle. Stir in the vinegar and add a little more salt, pepper and vinegar, if you like. Serve the lamb, beans and cooking liquid sprinkled with rosemary.

GREEK LAMB SHANKS IN TOMATO & GARLIC SAUCE

PREPARATION TIME: 15 minutes
COOKING TIME: 10 hours on LOW   **SERVES 4**

4 lamb shanks, about 14 ounces each

2 tablespoons dry oregano

2⅔ cups tomato puree

1 large head of garlic, separated into cloves and peeled

1 large onion, finely chopped

1 red bell pepper, halved lengthwise, seeded and sliced

salt and freshly ground black pepper

oregano or cilantro leaves, to serve

½ cup drained and crumbled feta cheese, to serve

2 tablespoons pine nuts, toasted (see page 170), to serve

sautéed potatoes, to serve

Season the lamb shanks with salt and pepper and put them in the slow cooker. Sprinkle the dry oregano over. Pour the tomato puree over, using a spoon to smooth it over the exposed part of the lamb shanks. The lamb will not be completely covered with liquid. Push the garlic down between the lamb shanks, then push in the onion and pepper and season lightly with salt and pepper.

Cover the cooker with the lid and cook on LOW 10 hours until the lamb is tender and starting to fall off the bones.

Transfer the lamb shanks and pepper slices to shallow bowls. Use a wooden spoon to smash the garlic into the side of the container and stir into the sauce. Add a little more salt and pepper, if you like. Spoon the sauce over the lamb shanks. Sprinkle with oregano, feta and toasted pine nuts and serve with sautéed potatoes.

CLASSIC BEEF STEW WITH CHEESE & HERB DUMPLINGS

PREPARATION TIME: 25 minutes, plus making the stock (optional) and dumplings
COOKING TIME: 4½ hours on HIGH   **SERVES 4**

4 cups chopped mixed root vegetables, such as carrots, celery root, parsnip or rutabaga, chopped

1 potato, such as Yukon Gold, about 7 ounces, chopped

2 bay leaves, torn

1 tablespoon dry thyme or dry parsley

1¾ pounds beef chuck or other stewing beef, trimmed of fat and cut into large chunks

2 tablespoons all-purpose flour

1 tablespoon dry mustard powder

2 tablespoons sunflower oil, plus extra if needed

1 celery stick, thinly sliced

1 onion, chopped

4 garlic cloves, finely chopped

3½ cups Beef Stock (see page 168) or store-bought stock, plus extra if needed

2 tablespoons Worcestershire sauce

1 recipe quantity Cheese & Herb Dumplings (see page 169)

4 tablespoons cornstarch (optional)

salt and freshly ground black pepper

chopped parsley leaves, to serve

Put the root vegetables, potato, bay leaves and thyme in the slow cooker. Put the beef in a bowl and season with salt and pepper. Add the flour and mustard powder. Toss gently, making sure the beef is coated in the flour mixture. Shake off and reserve any excess mixture.

Heat the oil in a large skillet over high heat. Lower the heat to medium, add the beef and fry 5 to 8 minutes until brown on all sides, working in batches to avoid overcrowding the pan and adding extra oil, if necessary. Use a slotted spoon to transfer the beef to the cooker as it browns, then sprinkle the reserved flour mixture over.

Pour off any excess fat from the pan, leaving about 1 tablespoon. Add the celery and onion and fry, stirring, 2 minutes. Add the garlic and fry 1 to 3 minutes longer until the onion is soft. Add the stock and Worcestershire sauce and bring to a boil, scraping the bottom of the pan, then pour the mixture into the cooker and season.

Cover the cooker with the lid and cook on HIGH 3½ hours. Quickly add the dumplings—they will sink, but rise to the surface as they cook. For a slightly thicker stew, put the cornstarch in a bowl and stir in 2 tablespoons cold water until smooth. Stir the cornstarch paste into the cooking liquid, then re-cover the cooker as quickly as possible and cook 1 hour until the dumplings have risen and are cooked through. Discard the bay leaves and add more salt and pepper, if you like. Serve sprinkled with parsley.

7

GREEK SPICED BEEF & ONION STEW

When you look down the list of ingredients you might think some stock has been missed off the list, but it hasn't. The small amount of added liquid and the cooking juices combine to make a thick, fragrant sauce.

PREPARATION TIME: 25 minutes
COOKING TIME: 7 hours on LOW   **SERVES 4**

4 tablespoons olive oil, plus extra if needed

1 pound shallots or pearl onions, peeled and an "X" cut in the bottom of each

4 large garlic cloves, halved

1¾ pounds boneless beef leg, trimmed of fat and cut into large chunks

4 bay leaves

3 cinnamon sticks

¼ teaspoon ground cloves

¼ teaspoon ground nutmeg, or to taste

2 tablespoons red wine vinegar

1 pound tomatoes, grated and skins discarded

4 tablespoons tomato paste

a pinch sugar

salt and freshly ground black pepper

chopped mint or cilantro leaves, to serve

boiled potatoes, to serve

Heat 2 tablespoons of the oil in a large skillet over high heat. Lower the heat to medium, add the shallots and fry, stirring, 3 to 5 minutes until just starting to turn golden. Add the garlic and stir 1 to 2 minutes longer. Use a slotted spoon to transfer the shallots and garlic to the slow cooker.

Heat the remaining oil in the pan. Add the beef and fry 3 to 5 minutes until brown on all sides, working in batches to avoid overcrowding the pan and adding extra oil, if necessary. Transfer the beef to the cooker as it browns.

Just before the final batch of beef finishes browning, add the bay leaves, cinnamon sticks, cloves and nutmeg and stir 30 seconds until fragrant. Add the the vinegar and tomatoes and stir until the vinegar evaporates.

Transfer the beef mixture to the cooker. Put the tomato paste and 4 tablespoons water in a small bowl and stir until dissolved, then stir into the beef mixture. Stir in the sugar and season with salt and pepper. The beef and onions will not be completely covered with liquid.

Cover the cooker with the lid and cook on LOW 7 hours until the beef is tender. Remove and discard the bay leaves and cinnamon sticks, and add a little more salt and pepper, if you like. Serve sprinkled with mint, and with boiled potatoes.

IRAQI BEEF DAUBE

PREPARATION TIME: 10 minutes, plus making the stock (optional) and 5 minutes resting
COOKING TIME: 5 hours on HIGH **SERVES 4**

1¾-pound piece chuck steak, tied
8 allspice berries or ½ teaspoon ground allspice, or to taste
6 cloves
6 large garlic cloves, sliced lengthwise
2 dry limes, slit open on one side
8 black peppercorns, very lightly crushed
1 cinnamon stick
2 cups tomato puree
½ cup Beef Stock (see page 168) or store-bought stock
salt and freshly ground black pepper
chopped cilantro leaves, to serve
pilaf, to serve (optional)

Make deep slits all over the beef and push the allspice berries, cloves and garlic into the slits.

Put the beef in the slow cooker with the dry limes, peppercorns and cinnamon stick. Add the tomato puree and stock and season with salt and pepper.

Cover the cooker with the lid and cook on HIGH 5 hours until the beef is tender. Remove the beef, wrap in foil and leave to rest for 5 minutes.

Meanwhile, remove and discard the cinnamon stick and dry limes and add a little more salt and pepper, if you like. Re-cover the cooker to keep the sauce warm.

Slice the beef, sprinkle with cilantro and serve with the cooking liquid spooned over the top, and with pilaf.

ONE-STEP BEEF STEW

PREPARATION TIME: 10 minutes
COOKING TIME: 10 hours on LOW **SERVES 4**

3 cups peeled and seeded butternut squash cut into large chunks
2 cups scrubbed and chopped small waxy potatoes
1 fennel head, chopped
1 onion, chopped
4 garlic cloves, chopped
2 tablespoons dry thyme
1½ pounds boneless beef shin, cut into large chunks
1 can (15-oz.) crushed tomatoes
2 tablespoons tomato paste
2 bay leaves, torn
salt and freshly ground black pepper
chopped parsley leaves, to serve

Put the squash, potatoes, fennel, onion, garlic and thyme in the slow cooker. Add the beef, crushed tomatoes and tomato paste, then tuck the bay leaves among the pieces of beef. Spoon 4 tablespoons water over and season with salt and pepper. The ingredients will not be completely covered with liquid.

Cover the cooker with the lid and cook on LOW 10 hours.

Remove and discard the bay leaves. Add more salt and pepper, if you like. Serve sprinkled with parsley.

BEEF BORSCHT

PREPARATION TIME: 15 minutes
COOKING TIME: 11½ hours on LOW,
   plus 30 minutes on HIGH   **SERVES 4**

1¾ pounds piece of boneless beef shin
4 teaspoons caraway seeds
2 large tomatoes, chopped
4 bay leaves
4 large raw beets, peeled and halved
4 garlic cloves, crushed
2 celery sticks, chopped
2 onions, chopped
2 carrots, 1 chopped and 1 grated
4 tablespoons red wine vinegar, plus extra to taste
2 tablespoons soft light brown sugar, plus extra
   to taste
2 tablespoons tomato paste
1¼ cups cored and shredded white cabbage
salt and freshly ground black pepper

Put the beef, caraway seeds, tomatoes, bay leaves, beets, garlic, celery, onions, chopped carrot, vinegar, sugar and tomato paste in the slow cooker and season. Pour 4 cups boiling water over, stirring. All the vegetables might not be covered with water.

Cover the cooker with the lid and cook on LOW 11½ hours until the beef is tender. Remove the beef from the cooker and leave to cool slightly.

Strain the cooking liquid into a bowl, pressing down on the vegetables. Discard the solids. Skim any excess fat from the the cooking liquid. Return the liquid to the cooker and add the cabbage and grated carrot. Switch the cooker to HIGH, re-cover and cook 30 minutes until the vegetables are tender. When the meat is cool enough to handle, remove and discard the skin and any gristle, then thinly slice and keep warm. When the vegetables are tender, add a little more vinegar or sugar, if you like. Serve with the beef.

BARBECUED BEEF SANDWICHES

PREPARATION TIME: 5 minutes, plus making the
   barbecue sauce (optional)
COOKING TIME: 10 hours on LOW
MAKES 8 SANDWICHES

1½ pounds boneless beef chuck or other stewing beef,
   cut into large chunks
1 cup Barbecue Sauce (see page 33) or bottled sauce
   of your choice
1 dill pickle, quartered lengthwise
salt and freshly ground black pepper
8 hamburger buns, cut in half, to serve
potato chips, to serve (optional)

Put the beef, barbecue sauce and dill pickle in the slow cooker and season with salt and pepper, then stir the ingredients together.

Cover the cooker with the lid and cook on LOW 10 hours. Remove and discard the dill pickle quarters. Use a slotted spoon to remove the beef from the cooker, leaving behind as much sauce as possible. Leave the beef to rest 5 minutes. Re-cover the cooker to keep the sauce warm.

Use two forks to shred the beef. Return the meat to the sauce and stir until combined. Serve hot or at room temperature, spooned on to hamburger buns, and with potato chips, if you like.

BEEF BURRITOS

PREPARATION TIME: 20 minutes
COOKING TIME: 10 hours on Low **SERVES 4**

4 large garlic cloves, peeled

1 tablespoon dry oregano

1 tablespoon sweet paprika

1 tablespoon ground cumin

2 teaspoons ground coriander

2 tablespoons sunflower oil

1½ pounds skirt steak, halved lengthwise,
then quartered

3 cups coarsely chopped tomatoes

2 red bell peppers, halved lengthwise, seeded and
coarsely chopped

4 tablespoons tomato puree

1 teaspoon hot pickled jalapeño chilies, or to taste

several cilantro sprigs, leaves and stems separated,
with the stems tied together

1 bay leaf

8 flour tortillas

salt and freshly ground black pepper

FILLINGS (OPTIONAL)

coarsely grated cheddar or Monterey Jack cheese

pitted black olives, sliced

skinned and seeded tomatoes, thinly sliced

shredded romaine lettuce

Put the garlic on a cutting board, lightly sprinkle with salt and use the tip of a knife to crush into a paste. Transfer the paste to a small bowl and stir in the oregano, paprika, cumin, ground coriander and oil. Use your hands to rub the mixture all over the pieces of steak, then season with salt and pepper.

Put the tomatoes, peppers, tomato puree, pickled chilies, cilantro stems and bay leaf in the slow cooker and top with the pieces of steak.

Cover the cooker with the lid and cook on LOW 10 hours until the meat is very tender. Remove the steak from the cooker, wrap in foil and leave to rest at least 10 minutes. Remove and discard the bay leaf and cilantro stems. Re-cover the cooker to keep the sauce warm.

Meanwhile, heat the oven to 350°F. Wrap the tortillas in foil and heat 10 to 15 minutes until hot. (Alternatively, wrap in plastic wrap and warm in a microwave on HIGH 30 to 45 seconds.)

Use two forks to shred the steak, then stir the meat into the sauce and season with a little more salt and pepper, if you like.

To assemble a burrito, spoon the beef filling down the middle of one tortilla, using a slotted spoon. Add any or all of the toppings, if you like, and sprinkle with cilantro leaves. Roll up the tortilla, then repeat to make 7 more burritos. Serve hot.

NEW ENGLAND POT ROAST

PREPARATION TIME: 20 minutes, plus making the stock and horseradish cream (optional)
COOKING TIME: 2 hours on HIGH, plus 8 hours on LOW   **SERVES 4**

2¼ pounds boneless beef brisket or silverside, rolled and tied

2 tablespoons all-purpose flour

2 tablespoons sunflower oil

8 small waxy potatoes, scrubbed and halved or quartered, if large

4 large garlic cloves, finely chopped

2 bay leaves

2 red onions, sliced

2 large carrots, sliced

2 rutabagas, quartered

1 cup Beef Stock (see page 168) or store-bought stock

salt and freshly ground black pepper

1 recipe quantity Horseradish & Dill Cream (see page 173), to serve (optional)

Season the brisket with salt and pepper, then use your hands to rub the flour all over the meat. Heat the oil in a large skillet over high heat. Lower the heat to medium, add the brisket and fry 5 to 8 minutes, turning once, until brown all over.

Transfer the brisket to the slow cooker, then add the potatoes, garlic, bay leaves, red onions, carrots and rutabagas. Pour the stock over and season lightly with salt and pepper. The vegetables will not be completely covered with liquid.

Cover the cooker with the lid. Cook on HIGH 2 hours, then switch the cooker to LOW and cook 8 hours longer until the beef and vegetables are tender. Transfer the brisket, potatoes, carrots and rutabagas to a large plate, then cover with foil and keep warm.

Strain the cooking liquid into a small saucepan, pressing down on the onions to extract as much flavor as possible. Bring to a boil over high heat, and boil 5 minutes until it reduces slightly and the flavors are concentrated. Add a little more salt and pepper, if you like.

Carve the brisket, then spoon the onion sauce over the brisket and vegetables and serve with Horseradish and Dill Cream, if you like.

GERMAN SAUERBRATEN

PREPARATION TIME: 40 minutes, plus cooling, 3 to 4 days marinating, plus making the stock (optional)
COOKING TIME: 2¼ hours on HIGH, plus 7¾ hours on LOW   **SERVES 4**

2¼ pounds boneless beef brisket, not rolled

4 tablespoons all-purpose flour

2 tablespoons sunflower oil

2 onions, chopped

1 carrot, chopped

1 celery stick, chopped

1½ cups Beef Stock (see page 168)
or store-bought stock

8 gingersnap biscuits, crumbled

salt and freshly ground black pepper

mashed potatoes, to serve

red cabbage cooked with apples, to serve

MARINADE

2 cups dry red wine

½ cup red wine vinegar

2 onions, sliced

1 carrot, sliced

8 juniper berries, lightly crushed

8 allspice berries, lightly crushed, or ½ teaspoon
ground allspice

8 black peppercorns, lightly crushed

8 cloves

2 bay leaves

To make the marinade, put all of the ingredients in a saucepan with ½ cup water. Bring to a boil over high heat. Lower the heat to low and simmer 15 minutes. Leave to cool completely. Put the brisket in a nonmetallic bowl and pour the marinade over. Cover and marinate in the refrigerator 3 to 4 days, turning the meat twice a day.

Remove the beef from the marinade and reserve the marinade. Pat the beef dry, season with salt and pepper and rub 2 tablespoons of the flour all over the meat. Heat the oil in a skillet over high heat. Lower the heat to medium, add the beef and fry 3 to 5 minutes until brown. Transfer to the slow cooker.

Pour off any excess fat in the pan, leaving about 1 tablespoon. Add the onions, carrot and celery and fry, stirring, 3 to 5 minutes until the onion is soft. Transfer the vegetables to the cooker. Strain the reserved marinade into the pan, discarding the solids. Add the stock and bring to a boil, then boil until it reduces by half. Pour over the brisket.

Cover the cooker with the lid and cook on HIGH 2 hours, then switch the cooker to LOW and cook 7¾ hours until the beef is tender. Remove the beef, cover and keep warm. Put the remaining flour and 4 tablespoons of the cooking liquid in a small bowl and stir until smooth. Stir the paste into the cooking liquid with the gingersnaps. Switch the cooker to HIGH, re-cover and cook 15 minutes until the sauce is thicker, then stir. Carve the beef. Strain the sauce, pressing down firmly on the vegetables, then discard the solids. Spoon the sauce over the beef and serve with mashed potatoes and red cabbage.

CUBAN ROPA VIEJA

Flank steak is the ideal cut for this rich stew. The recipe is called "old clothes," because the tender steak is shredded like rags just before serving.

PREPARATION TIME: 15 minutes
COOKING TIME: 10 hours on LOW   **SERVES 4**

1½-pound piece flank steak, halved lengthwise, then quartered

2 tablespoons olive oil

2 green bell peppers, halved lengthwise, seeded and sliced

1 large onion, sliced

4 large garlic cloves, chopped

2 teaspoons ground cumin

1 teaspoon ground cinnamon

a pinch ground cloves

1 can (15-oz.) crushed tomatoes

2 tablespoons tomato paste

1 bay leaf

1 habañero or other hot chili, seeded if you like, and thinly sliced

½ cup green olives, pitted and sliced

2 tablespoons drained capers in brine, rinsed

salt and freshly ground black pepper

chopped cilantro leaves, to serve

cooked long-grain white rice, to serve

Season the steak with salt and pepper and leave to one side. Heat the oil in a large skillet over high heat. Lower the heat to medium, add the peppers and onion and fry, stirring, 2 minutes. Add the garlic, cumin, cinnamon and cloves and stir 1 to 2 minutes longer until the onions are soft.

Add the crushed tomatoes, tomato paste, bay leaf and chili and season lightly with salt and pepper. Bring to a boil, stirring, then pour the mixture into the slow cooker and top with the pieces of steak.

Cover the cooker with the lid and cook on LOW 10 hours until the meat is very tender. Remove the steak from the cooker, wrap in foil and leave to rest 10 minutes. Meanwhile, remove and discard the bay leaf, then add the olives and capers to the sauce. Re-cover the cooker and heat through.

Use two forks to shred the beef, then stir the meat into the sauce and add a little more salt and pepper, if you like. Sprinkle with cilantro and serve with rice.

TWO-COURSE ITALIAN BEEF

Beef shin is one of those underrated, inexpensive cuts perfectly transformed by the slow cooker. It's an ideal choice for this Italian-inspired, two-course meal.

PREPARATION TIME: 10 minutes, plus making the salsa verde
COOKING TIME: 1¼ hours on HIGH, plus 8¾ hours on LOW · **SERVES 4**

1¾ pounds boneless beef shin, tied lengthwise

2 bay leaves, torn

2 fennel bulbs, quartered

1 celery stick with leaves, quartered

1 large onion, quartered

1 tablespoon fennel seeds

4 tablespoons small soup pasta, such as stars or loops

salt and freshly ground black pepper

freshly grated Parmesan cheese, to serve

1 recipe quantity Salsa Verde (see page 174), to serve

mixed green salad, to serve

Put the beef, bay leaves, fennel, celery, onion and fennel seeds in the slow cooker, tucking the vegetables down around the beef, if necessary. Fill the container with water, leaving a 1-inch gap at the top of the pot, and season with salt and pepper.

Cover the cooker with the lid. Cook on HIGH 1 hour, then switch the cooker to LOW and cook 8¾ hours longer until the beef is tender.

When the beef is almost tender, heat the oven to 300°F. Use a large metal spoon to skim any excess fat from the surface of the cooking liquid. When the beef is tender, transfer to a rimmed heatproof plate and ladle enough cooking liquid over the top to keep the meat moist. Cover with foil and keep warm in the oven until required.

Strain the cooking liquid into a bowl, reserving the fennel and discarding the other solids, then return the liquid to the cooker and switch the cooker to HIGH. Finely chop the cooked fennel. Add the fennel and pasta to the cooker, then season with a little more salt and pepper, if you like.

Re-cover the cooker and cook 15 minutes longer until the pasta is tender. Serve the broth, fennel and pasta as a first course sprinkled with grated Parmesan. For a second course, thinly slice the beef and serve with Salsa Verde and a salad.

(7)

BEEF & EGGPLANT TAGINE

This is a very rich and filling dish. When friends come for dinner, I simply serve it with a bowl of couscous, followed by fruit. Orange slices dusted with ground ginger and ground cardamom are especially good.

PREPARATION TIME: 25 minutes, plus making the stock (optional)
COOKING TIME: 7 hours on LOW   **SERVES 4**

1¾ pounds boneless beef shoulder, trimmed of fat and cut into large chunks

2 tablespoons olive oil, plus extra if needed

2½ cups peeled and chopped eggplant

8 dates or ready-to-eat dry apricots

2 preserved lemons, sliced

1 fennel bulb, sliced

4 large garlic cloves, finely chopped

2 bay leaves

2 teaspoons fennel seeds

1 tablespoon ground cumin

1 tablespoon ras el hanout

2 teaspoons dry thyme

2 tablespoons tomato paste

1 cup Beef Stock (see page 168), store-bought stock or water

salt and freshly ground black pepper

chopped cilantro leaves, to serve

pomegranate seeds (optional), to serve

cooked couscous, to serve

Season the beef with salt and pepper. Heat the oil in a large skillet over high heat. Lower the heat to medium, add the beef and fry 3 to 5 minutes until brown on all sides, working in batches to avoid overcrowding the pan and adding extra oil, if necessary. Use a slotted spoon to transfer the beef to the slow cooker as it browns. Add the eggplant, dates and preserved lemons to the cooker.

Pour off any excess fat from the pan, leaving about 1 tablespoon. Add the fennel and fry, stirring, 2 minutes. Add the garlic and fry 1 to 3 minutes longer until the fennel is soft. Add the bay leaves, fennel seeds, cumin, ras el hanout and thyme and fry 30 to 60 seconds until fragrant.

Add the tomato paste and stock and season lightly with salt and pepper. Bring to a boil, stirring, then pour the mixture into the cooker and stir well.

Cover the cooker with the lid and cook on LOW 7 hours until the beef is tender. Remove and discard the bay leaves, then stir well and add a little more salt and pepper, if you like. Sprinkle with cilantro and pomegranate seeds, if you like, and serve with couscous.

MASSAMAN BEEF & POTATO CURRY

One of the reasons I like making this fragrant, souplike Thai curry is that it really is a complete meal-in-a-pot. It contains potatoes, so I don't even have to think about cooking any rice.

PREPARATION TIME: 10 minutes, plus making the curry paste, and stock (optional)
COOKING TIME: 8 hours on LOW   **SERVES 4**

10 ounces small waxy potatoes, peeled and halved if large

1¾ pounds boneless beef leg, trimmed of fat and cut into large chunks

9 ounces Thai or small shallots, peeled

9 ounces green beans, topped and tailed

1 recipe quantity Massaman Curry Paste (see page 170)

½ cup Beef Stock (see page 168) or store-bought stock, boiling

1 cup coconut milk

1 kaffir lime leaf

salt and freshly ground black pepper

chopped cilantro leaves, to serve

chopped salted peanuts, to serve

Put the potatoes in the slow cooker, then add the beef, shallots and green beans.

Dissolve the curry paste in the stock, then pour it over the beef and vegetables. Pour the coconut milk over, add the lime leaf, season with salt and pepper and stir. The beef and vegetables will not be completely covered with liquid.

Cover the cooker with the lid and cook on LOW 8 hours until the beef and vegetables are tender. Add a little more salt and pepper, if you like. Sprinkle with cilantro and peanuts and serve.

(3)

BOBOTIE

PREPARATION TIME: 25 minutes, plus 10 minutes standing
COOKING TIME: 2 hours on LOW, plus 1 hour on HIGH   **SERVES 4**

½ cup dry bread crumbs

2 tablespoons sunflower oil

1 onion, finely chopped

4 large garlic cloves, finely chopped

1 tablespoon Madras curry powder, or to taste

2 teaspoons apple pie spice

1 tablespoon Italian mixed herbs

1½ pounds lean ground beef, or a mixture of ground beef and ground lamb

½ cup ready-to-eat dry apricots, halved

3 bay leaves

1 green chili, seeded and finely chopped (optional)

4 tablespoons golden raisins or raisins

finely grated zest of 1 large lemon

salt and freshly ground black pepper

TOPPING

2 extra-large eggs

1¼ cups milk

¼ teaspoon turmeric

salt

Put the bread crumbs in a bowl, add just enough water to cover and leave to soak. Meanwhile, heat 1 tablespoon of the oil in a large skillet over high heat. Lower the heat to medium, add the onion and fry, stirring, 2 minutes. Add the garlic, curry powder and apple pie spice and fry 1 to 3 minutes longer until the onion is soft. Use a slotted spoon to transfer the mixture to the slow cooker, then sprinkle with the mixed herbs.

Heat the remaining oil in the pan. Add the beef and fry, breaking up the meat, until brown all over. Use a slotted spoon to transfer the beef to the cooker, leaving behind as much oil as possible. Add the dry apricots, bay leaves, chili, if using, golden raisins and lemon zest to the cooker and season with salt and pepper. Squeeze the bread crumbs to remove as much water as possible, then add to the cooker and stir well. Cover with the lid and cook on LOW 2 hours.

Five minutes before the end of the cooking time, make the topping. Mix all of the ingredients in a bowl and season with salt. Remove the cooker lid and stir the beef mixture. Skim any excess fat from the cooking liquid, then remove and discard the bay leaves. Add a little more salt and pepper, if you like, then pour over the topping mixture.

Quickly cover the top of the slow cooker with plastic wrap and re-cover with the lid. Switch the cooker to HIGH and cook 1 hour longer until the topping is set. Remove the plastic wrap and leave the bobotie to stand 10 minutes until the topping firms up. Serve straight from the container.

CURRIED GROUND BEEF & PEAS

PREPARATION TIME: 20 minutes, plus making the stock and raita (optional)
COOKING TIME: 4 hours on LOW, plus 15 minutes on HIGH   **SERVES 4**

2 tablespoons sunflower oil

2 cinnamon sticks

1 onion, finely chopped

1½-inch piece gingerroot, peeled and finely chopped

4 garlic cloves, finely chopped

2 green chilies, seeded and finely chopped

1 tablespoon curry powder

2 teaspoons ground cardamom

1 teaspoon ground coriander

1 teaspoon ground cumin

½ teaspoon ground cloves

¼ teaspoon cayenne pepper, or to taste

¼ teaspoon turmeric

1½ pounds lean ground beef

1 can (15-oz.) crushed tomatoes

4 tablespoons tomato puree

½ cup Beef Stock (see page 168), Vegetable Stock (see page 169) or store-bought stock

1 bay leaf

1⅓ cups frozen peas, thawed

salt and freshly ground black pepper

chopped cilantro leaves, to serve

warm naan breads, to serve

1 recipe quantity Cucumber & Tomato Raita (see page 172), to serve (optional)

Heat 1 tablespoon of the oil in a large skillet over medium-high heat. Add the cinnamon sticks and fry, stirring, about 30 seconds until fragrant. Use a slotted spoon to remove the cinnamon sticks from the pan and leave to one side.

Lower the heat to medium. Add the onion to the pan and fry 2 minutes. Add the ginger, garlic, chilies, curry powder and spices and fry 1 to 3 minutes longer until the onion is soft. Use a slotted spoon to transfer the mixture to the slow cooker.

Heat the remaining oil in the pan. Add the beef and fry, breaking up the meat, until brown all over. Use a slotted spoon to transfer the beef to the cooker, leaving behind as much oil as possible. Add the crushed tomatoes, tomato puree, stock, bay leaf and fried cinnamon sticks to the cooker and stir well, then season with salt and pepper.

Cover the cooker with the lid and cook on LOW 4 hours, then stir in the peas. Switch the cooker to HIGH, re-cover and cook 15 minutes until the peas are tender. Remove and discard the bay leaf and cinnamon sticks and add a little more salt and pepper, if you like. Sprinkle with cilantro and serve with naan breads and Cucumber & Tomato Raita, if you like.

9

RIBS BRAISED IN RED WINE

PREPARATION TIME: 30 minutes, plus making the stock (optional)
COOKING TIME: 9 hours on LOW   **SERVES 4**

3½ pounds bone-in beef short ribs in large pieces

2 tablespoons olive oil, plus extra if needed

2 carrots, chopped

1 celery stick, finely chopped

1 onion, chopped

2 cups Beef Stock (see page 168) or store-bought stock

3 cups full-bodied red wine

8 black peppercorns, crushed

6 garlic cloves, finely chopped

2 bay leaves, torn

3 tablespoons herbes de Provence or Italian mixed herbs

3 tablespoons butter, soft

3 tablespoons all-purpose flour

salt and freshly ground black pepper

mashed potatoes, to serve (optional)

Season the ribs with salt and pepper. Heat the oil in a large skillet over high heat. Lower the heat to medium, add the ribs and fry until brown on all sides, working in batches to avoid overcrowding the pan and adding extra oil, if necessary. Transfer the ribs to the slow cooker as they brown.

Pour off any excess fat from the pan, leaving about 1 tablespoon. Add the carrots, celery and onion and fry, stirring, 3 to 5 minutes until the onion is soft. Add the stock, wine, peppercorns, garlic, bay leaves and herbs and season with salt and pepper. Bring to a boil, stirring, until the liquid is reduced by half. Pour the mixture into the cooker. The ribs will not be completely covered with liquid.

Cover the cooker with the lid. Cook on LOW 9 hours until the meat and vegetables are tender and the meat comes away from the bones easily. Remove the meat from the cooker, then wrap in foil and keep warm. Discard any bones and the bay leaves.

Beat together the butter and flour. Strain the cooking liquid through a fine strainer into a saucepan, pressing down to extract as much flavor as possible. Skim any excess fat from the cooking liquid, and bring to a boil. Gradually whisk in the butter mixture. Boil, whisking continuously, over high heat 5 minutes until the sauce reduces to about 2 cups and thickens. Add a little more salt and pepper, if you like. Serve the beef with the sauce spooned over the top, and with mashed potatoes, if you like.

MEAT & POULTRY

KOREAN RIBS & DAIKON

The meat on the ribs takes on an extra dimension of flavor as it absorbs the sharp peppery flavor of the daikon. Cooking the white daikon in large chunks ensures that it doesn't overcook, so it can be diced and served alongside the rich meat.

PREPARATION TIME: 15 minutes, plus pickling the bean sprouts (optional)
COOKING TIME: 5 hours on HIGH   **SERVES 4**

1 cup soy sauce

8 scallions, finely chopped, plus extra to serve

2-inch piece gingerroot, finely grated

8 garlic cloves, very finely chopped

4 tablespoons dark brown sugar

1 tablespoon sesame oil

3½ pounds bone-in beef short ribs in large pieces

2 cups daikon cut into thick pieces

salt and freshly ground black pepper

2 tablespoons sesame seeds, toasted (see page 170), to serve

Pickled Bean Sprouts (see page 173) or kimchi, to serve

Put the soy sauce, scallions, ginger, garlic, brown sugar, oil and ½ cup water in the slow cooker, stirring to dissolve the sugar. Season with pepper. Add the ribs and spoon the liquid over the top, making sure the ribs are coated in the soy sauce mixture. Add the daikon, tucking it down around the ribs. The ribs and daikon will not be completely covered with liquid.

Cover the cooker with the lid and cook on HIGH 5 hours until the meat is tender and comes away from the bones easily.

When the meat is tender, season with salt, if needed, and add a little more pepper, if you like. Remove the daikon from the cooking liquid and dice it. Use a large metal spoon to skim any excess fat from the surface of the cooking liquid, and remove and discard any bones.

Spoon the cooking liquid over the beef, sprinkle with toasted sesame seeds and scallions and serve with the daikon and Pickled Bean Sprouts.

SPANISH MEATBALLS

PREPARATION TIME: 30 minutes, plus making the tomato sauce (optional)
COOKING TIME: 4 hours on LOW, plus 15 minutes on HIGH **SERVES 4**

¼ cup pine nuts, toasted (see page 170)

9 ounces lean ground beef

9 ounces lean ground pork

½ cup dry bread crumbs

4 large garlic cloves, minced

2 eggs, beaten

3 tablespoons finely chopped parsley leaves

¼ teaspoon ground cinnamon

3 tablespoons all-purpose flour, for dusting, plus extra if needed

1 tablespoon garlic-flavored olive oil, plus extra if needed

1¾ cups frozen peas, thawed

salt and freshly ground black pepper

cooked short-grain white rice, to serve

SAUCE

1 large onion, finely chopped

4 large garlic cloves, crushed

2 cups skinned and diced fresh chorizo

2½ cups Easy Tomato Sauce (see page 34), bottled tomato sauce or tomato puree

To make the meatballs, put the pine nuts, beef, pork, bread crumbs, garlic, eggs, parsley and cinnamon in a bowl and season with salt and pepper. Combine the ingredients, using wet hands, making sure the pine nuts and parsley are evenly distributed. Divide the mixture into 2 equal portions, then roll each half into 10 balls. Transfer the meat balls to a floured plate.

Heat the oil in a skillet over high heat. Lower the heat to medium, add the meatballs and fry 3 to 5 minutes, until brown all over, working in batches and adding extra oil, if necessary. Transfer the meat balls to the slow cooker as they brown.

To make the sauce, pour off any excess fat from the pan, leaving about 1 tablespoon. Add the onion and fry, stirring, 2 minutes. Add the garlic and chorizo and fry 1 to 3 minutes longer until the onion is soft. Add the tomato sauce and bring to a boil, scraping the bottom of the pan, then pour the mixture into the cooker.

Cover the cooker and cook on LOW 4 hours. Test the meatballs are cooked through by cutting one in half. Return the meatball to the cooker and add the peas. Switch the cooker to HIGH, re-cover and cook 15 minutes until the peas are tender. Add a little more salt and pepper, if you like. Serve the meatballs and sauce spooned over rice.

COOK'S TIP
To check for seasoning in the meatballs, fry a small amount of the mixture before it is shaped and taste. This way you can add extra salt and/or pepper before the meatballs are fried.

10

ISRAELI SABBATH BRISKET

PREPARATION TIME: 30 minutes
COOKING TIME: 2 hours on HIGH, plus 8 hours on LOW   **SERVES 4**

1½ pounds brisket, cut into large chunks

2 tablespoons olive oil, plus extra if needed

1 can (15-oz.) red kidney beans, drained and rinsed

8 small waxy potatoes, peeled and halved or quartered, if large

2 onions, chopped

4 garlic cloves, chopped

½ cup pearl barley

2 bay leaves

4 tablespoons dark brown sugar

2 tablespoons tomato paste

1 tablespoon dry thyme

1½ teaspoons sweet, smoked or hot paprika, or to taste

4 eggs, at room temperature

salt and freshly ground black pepper

chopped parsley leaves, to serve

Season the brisket with salt and pepper. Heat the oil in a large skillet over high heat. Lower the heat to medium, add the beef and fry 3 to 5 minutes until brown on all sides, working in batches to avoid overcrowding the pan and adding extra oil, if necessary. Use a slotted spoon to transfer the beef to the slow cooker. Add the beans and potatoes to the cooker.

Pour off any excess fat from the pan, leaving about 1 tablespoon. Lower the heat to low, add the onions and fry, stirring, 8 to 10 minutes until just starting to brown. Add the garlic and stir 1 minute. Transfer the onions and garlic to the cooker.

Add the barley, bay leaves, brown sugar, tomato paste, thyme and paprika to the cooker and season lightly with salt and pepper. Pour over just enough boiling water to cover all of the ingredients, then stir to dissolve the sugar and tomato paste.

Cover the cooker with the lid and cook on HIGH 2 hours, then switch the cooker to LOW and cook 7 hours longer. Add the eggs, gently pushing them down into the cooking liquid. Re-cover the cooker and cook 1 hour longer until the meat, barley and potatoes are tender.

Remove and discard the bay leaves and add a little more salt and pepper, if you like. Remove the eggs from the cooker, then shell them. Divide the eggs into bowls, then add a mixture of meat, potatoes and barley to each. Sprinkle with parsley and serve.

IRISH OX CHEEKS

PREPARATION TIME: 25 minutes
COOKING TIME: 6 hours on LOW,
    plus 30 minutes on HIGH   **SERVES 4**

2 ox cheeks, about 1 pound 2 ounces each, trimmed
    of fat and cut into large pieces
2 tablespoons all-purpose flour
1 tablespoon sunflower oil
4 tablespoons oat groats
6 juniper berries, tied in cheesecloth and crushed
1½ cups peeled, cored and diced parsnips
1 large leek, halved lengthwise, sliced and rinsed
2 large garlic cloves, chopped
1⅓ cups stout, ale or lager
1½ cups cored and shredded white cabbage
salt and freshly ground black pepper
boiled or mashed potatoes, to serve

Season the ox cheeks with salt and pepper and dust
with the flour. Heat the oil in a skillet over high heat.
Lower the heat to medium, add the cheeks and fry
3 to 5 minutes until brown. Transfer to the slow
cooker. Add the oats and juniper bundle, tucking
them between the meat. Add the parsnips.

Pour off any excess fat from the pan, leaving about
1 tablespoon. Add the leek and fry, stirring,
2 minutes. Add the garlic and fry 1 to 3 minutes.
Transfer the leek and garlic to the cooker, then pour
the stout over and season with pepper.

Cover the cooker and cook on LOW 6 hours until the
beef is tender. Remove the meat, wrap in foil and
keep warm. Discard the juniper bundle, then skim
any excess fat from the cooking liquid. Switch the
cooker to HIGH and add the cabbage. Re-cover and
cook 30 minutes until the oats are tender. Season
with salt and a little more pepper, if you like. Cut the
meat into bite-size pieces and serve with potatoes.

OXTAIL & FARRO

PREPARATION TIME: 10 minutes, plus making
    the stock (optional)
COOKING TIME: 10 hours on LOW   **SERVES 4**

1½ cups thickly sliced carrots
1 cup peeled parsnips cut into chunks
1 onion, finely chopped
2 tablespoons dry sage or thyme
3½ pound oxtail, cut into chunks
2½ cups Beef Stock (see page 168)
    or store-bought stock
2 tablespoons tomato paste
1 tablespoon Worcestershire sauce, plus extra to taste
4 tablespoons farro or pearl barley
salt and freshly ground black pepper
chopped parsley leaves, to serve
mashed potatoes, to serve

Put the carrots, parsnips and onion in the slow
cooker and sprinkle the sage over. Top with the
oxtail chunks. Pour the stock over, then stir in the
tomato paste and Worcestershire sauce and season
with pepper. Push the farro into the liquid, tucking
it down between the oxtail chunks. The oxtail will
not be completely covered with liquid.

Cover the cooker with the lid and cook on LOW 10
hours until the meat is very tender and starting to
fall off the bones.

Remove and discard any bones. Season with salt
and add a little more Worcestershire sauce and
pepper, if you like. Divide the oxtail and vegetables
into bowls. Spoon the farro and cooking liquid
over, sprinkle with parsley and serve with mashed
potatoes.

VEAL, FENNEL & RED PEPPER STEW

PREPARATION TIME: 25 minutes, plus making the stock and 20 minutes thickening time (optional)
COOKING TIME: 6½ hours on LOW   **SERVES 4**

1¾ pounds boneless veal shoulder, trimmed of fat and cut into large chunks

2 tablespoons all-purpose flour

2 tablespoons olive oil, plus extra if needed

2 fennel bulbs, chopped with the fronds reserved

4 large garlic cloves, finely chopped

4 tablespoons aniseed-flavored spirit

1 cup Vegetable Stock (see page 169) or store-bought stock

1 tablespoon dry dill

1 tablespoon fennel seeds, tied in a piece of cheesecloth and lightly crushed

4 large chargrilled, skinless red peppers in oil, drained and sliced

2 tablespoons cornstarch (optional)

salt and freshly ground black pepper

polenta or boiled potatoes, to serve

Put the the veal in a bowl and season with salt and pepper. Add the flour and toss gently, shaking off and reserving any excess flour. Heat the oil in a large skillet over high heat. Lower the heat to medium, add the veal and fry 5 to 8 minutes until brown, working in batches and adding extra oil, if necessary. Transfer the veal to the slow cooker, then sprinkle the reserved flour over.

Pour off any excess fat from the pan, leaving about 1 tablespoon. Add the fennel and fry, stirring, 2 minutes. Add the garlic and fry 1 to 3 minutes longer until the fennel is soft. Add the spirit, then carefully set it alight and allow the flames to flare up and die out. Transfer the fennel to the cooker, then add the stock and dill and stir well. Push the fennel seed bundle down between the pieces of veal. Season lightly with salt and pepper. The ingredients will not be completely covered with liquid.

Cover the cooker with the lid and cook on LOW 6 hours. Stir in the peppers. Re-cover the cooker and cook 30 minutes longer until the veal is tender. Use a slotted spoon to remove the veal and vegetables from the cooker, then wrap in foil and keep warm.

For a thicker sauce, put the cornstarch and 4 tablespoons cold water in a small bowl and stir until smooth, then stir the paste into the cooking liquid. Switch the cooker to HIGH, re-cover and cook 20 minutes until thickened.

Discard the fennel seed bundle and add a little more salt and pepper, if you like. Return the veal and vegetables to the cooker and heat through. Serve with polenta.

OSSO BUCO

PREPARATION TIME: 25 minutes, plus making the stock (optional), gremolata, and risotto (optional)
COOKING TIME: 2½ hours on HIGH **SERVES 4**

4 veal shank pieces, about 9 ounces each, and 1½ inches thick

1 tablespoon all-purpose flour

4 tablespoons olive oil, plus extra if needed

1 carrot, finely diced

1 celery stick, finely chopped

1 onion, finely chopped

2 garlic cloves, finely chopped

4 tablespoons dry red wine

2 teaspoons dry rosemary

1 cup Beef Stock (see page 168) or store-bought stock

1 cup tomato puree

1 strip lemon peel, pith removed

salt and freshly ground black pepper

1 recipe quantity Gremolata (see page 169), to serve

1 recipe quantity Saffron Risotto (see page 173), to serve (optional)

Season the veal shanks with salt and pepper, then dust with the flour, shaking off the excess. Heat 2 tablespoons of the oil in a large skillet over high heat. Lower the heat to medium, add the veal shanks and fry 5 to 8 minutes until brown on both sides, working in batches to avoid overcrowding the pan and adding extra oil, if necessary. Transfer the shanks to the slow cooker as they are brown.

Heat the remaining oil in the pan. Add the carrot, celery and onion and fry, stirring, 2 minutes. Add the garlic and fry 1 to 3 minutes longer until the onion is soft. Add the wine and rosemary and leave to bubble until the wine almost evaporates. Stir in the stock and tomato puree and bring to a boil, scraping the bottom of the pan, and boil until the liquid reduces by half. Add the lemon peel and season with salt and pepper. Pour over the veal shanks—they will not be completely covered with liquid.

Cover the cooker and cook on HIGH 2½ hours until the meat is tender.

When the veal shanks are tender, remove and discard the lemon peel and add a little more salt and pepper, if you like. Spoon the cooking liquid over the veal shanks, sprinkle with Gremolata and serve with Saffron Risotto, if you like.

FISH &
SHELLFISH

One of the unexpected discoveries of using a slow cooker is just how adept it is at cooking seafood. As you look through the diverse recipes in this chapter you'll find the selection includes both dishes that quietly simmer away, as well as quicker ones that are ready to eat in just over an hour, but still don't require much attention on your part. In either case, the gentle cooking of the slow cooker helps prevent the ultimate cooking disaster—overcooked seafood.

The transformation of hard, cardboardlike salt cod into tender, succulent fish has to be one of the miracles of the culinary world. To see how easily the slow cooker accomplishes this, try the Mediterranean Salt Cod recipe (see page 114).

For a retro dinner party appetizer that never fails to impress, try the delicious Salmon Terrine with Watercress Sauce (see page 116). It's ideal for entertaining because the terrine can be assembled in advance and be ready to cook just before your guests arrive. Then, as a bonus, if anyone is late, or you linger too long over drinks, you don't have to worry as the terrine will stay warm in the cooker.

◄ SALMON & SWEET POTATO CHOWDER (SEE PAGE 119)

MEDITERRANEAN SALT COD

PREPARATION TIME: 20 minutes, plus 24 hours soaking the cod and 30 minutes standing
COOKING TIME: 1 hour on HIGH plus 15 minutes on LOW   **SERVES 4**

14 ounces dry salt cod fillet

4 garlic cloves, crushed

2 bay leaves, torn

2 fennel bulbs, quartered

1 onion, sliced

½ lemon, sliced

½ tablespoon fennel seeds

4 tablespoons extra virgin olive oil, plus extra to serve

3 tablespoons milk

freshly ground black pepper

chopped parsley leaves, to serve

16 black olives, pitted and sliced, to serve

2 large chargrilled red peppers in oil, drained and sliced, to serve

slices of French bread, toasted, to serve

Put the cod in a nonmetallic bowl. Cover with cold water and leave to soak 24 hours, replacing the soaking water with fresh water 3 or 4 times.

One hour before the end of the soaking time, put the garlic, bay leaves, fennel, onion, lemon and fennel seeds in the slow cooker and pour 3 cups boiling water over.

Cover the cooker with the lid and cook on HIGH 1 hour until the flavors are blended.

Drain the salt cod and rinse well. Cut the cod into large pieces, if necessary. Add the rinsed cod to the cooker, flesh-side down. Switch the cooker to LOW, re-cover and cook 15 minutes. Switch the cooker off and leave the cod to stand in the cooking liquid 30 minutes, without lifting the lid.

Use a slotted spoon to remove the cod from the cooker and gently shake off any excess liquid. When the cod is cool enough to handle, wipe off the fennel seeds and flake the fish into large chunks, removing the skin and all small bones. Transfer three-quarters of the flesh to a food processor.

Heat the olive oil in a pan over high heat until hot. Add 1 tablespoon of the hot olive oil to the food processor and process the cod. Continue adding the olive oil, 1 tablespoon at a time, until a thick puree forms. Add the milk and process again. Gently stir in the remaining flaked cod, and season with pepper. Sprinkle with parsley, olives and peppers and serve with slices of toast drizzled with olive oil.

SALMON TERRINE

PREPARATION TIME: 20 minutes, plus 15 minutes chilling, 10 minutes standing and making the sauce
COOKING TIME: 1½ hours on LOW   **SERVES 4**

14 ounces boneless, skinless white fish, such as cod, haddock, monkfish, pollack and whiting, coarsely chopped with all pin bones removed

1 tablespoon butter, plus extra for greasing

¼ teaspoon salt

1 egg white

⅔ cup heavy cream

1 tablespoon dry dill

finely grated zest of 1 lemon

7 ounces boneless, skinless salmon fillets, about ¼ inch thick, cut into thin strips with all pin bones removed

salt and freshly ground black pepper

1 recipe quantity Watercress Sauce (see page 174)

Put an upturned heatproof saucer in the slow cooker. Grease a 2-cup bread pan or other suitable dish that will fit on top of the saucer with the cooker lid in place. Line the bottom of the pan with parchment paper, then grease the paper.

Puree the white fish in a blender or food processor until smooth. With the motor still running, add the butter and salt and continue blending until incorporated. Add the egg white and incorporate. Transfer the fish paste to a bowl, then cover and chill 15 minutes.

Slowly beat in the cream, 1 tablespoon at a time, until blended. Add the dill and lemon zest and season with salt and pepper. Spoon half of the mixture into the prepared pan and smooth the surface with a wet spatula. Arrange the salmon over the mixture. Very gently add the remaining white fish mixture and smooth the surface.

Cut out a piece of foil to cover the top of the pan with a ¼-inch overhang, then press it down over the edges of the pan. Put the pan on top of the saucer, then pour enough boiling water into the container to reach halfway up the sides of the pan.

Cover the cooker with the lid and cook on LOW 1½ hours until the terrine is set and comes away from the pan. Switch the cooker off and leave the terrine to stand 10 minutes. Remove the terrine from the cooker, then discard the foil and carefully pour out the cooking juices. Invert the terrine onto a plate and remove the tin and parchment paper. Cut into slices and serve with Watercress Sauce.

SALMON & SWEET POTATO CHOWDER

PREPARATION TIME: 20 minutes, plus making the stock (optional)
COOKING TIME: 4 hours 20 minutes on LOW   **SERVES 4**

1 tablespoon butter

1 tablespoon sunflower oil

1 celery stick, finely chopped

1 onion, finely chopped

4 tablespoons all-purpose flour

½ cup Fish Stock (see page 168), weak Vegetable Stock (see page 169) or store-bought stock

3 cups milk

2 cups diced sweet potatoes

2 bay leaves

1 long strip lemon peel, pith removed

1 tablespoon dry thyme

¼ teaspoon salt, or to taste

1½ pounds boneless, skinless salmon fillets, about 1 inch thick, cut into bite-size pieces

4 slices smoked bacon

freshly ground black pepper

finely chopped parsley leaves, to serve

smoked or sweet paprika, to serve

Melt the butter with the oil in a large skillet over high heat. Lower the heat to medium, add the celery and onion and fry, stirring, 3 to 5 minutes until the onion is soft. Sprinkle the flour over and stir 2 minutes to cook out the raw flavor. Pour the stock over and bring to a boil, stirring continuously to prevent lumps forming. The mixture will be very thick and pastelike.

Slowly stir in the milk. Add the sweet potatoes, bay leaves, lemon peel, thyme and salt, then season with pepper. Cover and bring to a boil, then pour the mixture into the slow cooker.

Cover the cooker with the lid and cook on LOW 4 hours until the sweet potatoes are tender. Gently stir in the salmon, re-cover and cook 20 minutes longer until the salmon is cooked through and flakes easily.

Meanwhile, preheat the broiler to high. When hot, broil the bacon 2 to 3 minutes on each side until cooked and crisp. Drain well on paper towels, then chop very finely. Wrap in foil and keep warm.

When the salmon is cooked, remove and discard the bay leaves and lemon peel, and add a little more salt and pepper, if you like. Sprinkle with bacon, parsley and paprika and serve.

KEDGEREE

PREPARATION TIME: 20 minutes, plus making the stock (optional) and at least 5 minutes standing
COOKING TIME: 1 hour 15 minutes on HIGH   **SERVES 4**

2 tablespoons sunflower oil

1 large onion, finely chopped

2 tablespoons hot or mild curry paste, to taste

3 cups Vegetable Stock (see page 169)
or store-bought stock

1½ cups easy-cook white rice

¼ teaspoon salt, or to taste

4 eggs, at room temperature

2 undyed smoked haddock fillets, about 10 ounces
each, skinned and cut into bite-size pieces

freshly ground black pepper

4 tablespoons chopped cilantro or parsley leaves,
to serve

mango chutney, to serve (optional)

Heat the oil in a saucepan over high heat. Lower the heat to low, add the onion and fry, stirring frequently, 8 to 10 minutes until golden brown. Stir in the curry paste and continue stirring 1 to 2 minutes until fragrant.

Add the stock, increase the heat to high and bring to a boil, then pour the mixture into the slow cooker. Stir in the rice, add the salt and season with pepper. Gently push the eggs into the rice. The eggs will not be completely covered with liquid.

Cover the cooker with the lid and cook on HIGH 1 hour. Gently stir the haddock into the rice. Turn the eggs over, quickly re-cover the cooker and cook 15 minutes longer until the rice is tender and the haddock is cooked through and flakes easily. Remove the eggs from the cooker and leave to cool slightly.

Switch the cooker off. Put a clean dish towel over the kedgeree, re-cover with the lid and leave to stand at least 5 minutes. The kedgeree can be left covered with the dish towel up to 30 minutes. Add a little more salt and pepper, if you like.

Just before serving, and when cool enough to handle, shell and coarsely chop the eggs. Sprinkle the kedgeree with the chopped eggs and cilantro, and serve with mango chutney, if you like.

CHIMICHURRI HADDOCK

PREPARATION TIME: 15 minutes, plus making the stock (optional)
COOKING TIME: 1 hour on HIGH, plus 12 minutes on LOW   **SERVES 4**

3½ cups Fish Stock (see page 168), weak Vegetable Stock (see page 169) or store-bought stock

2 bay leaves

1 fennel bulb, sliced

thinly pared peel of 1 lemon, pith removed

4 boneless, skinless haddock or cod fillets, about 5 ounces each and 1 inch thick

salt and freshly ground black pepper

lemon wedges, to serve

sautéed potatoes, to serve (optional)

CHIMICHURRI SAUCE

½ cup extra virgin olive oil, plus extra if needed

2 tablespoons lemon juice, plus extra to taste

2 to 4 large garlic cloves, finely chopped, to taste

1 red chili, seeded if you like, and finely sliced

2 tablespoons finely chopped cilantro leaves

2 tablespoons chopped parsley leaves

salt and freshly ground black pepper

Put the stock, bay leaves, fennel and lemon peel in the slow cooker and season with salt and pepper.

Cover the cooker with the lid and cook on HIGH 1 hour until the flavors blend.

Switch the cooker to LOW. Add the haddock, re-cover and cook 12 minutes until the haddock is cooked through and flakes easily. Use a fish slice to remove the fillets from the cooker, then pat dry with paper towels and transfer to plates.

Meanwhile, make the sauce. In a nonmetallic bowl, whisk together the olive oil, lemon juice, garlic and chili. Stir in the cilantro and parsley and season with salt and pepper. Add a little more lemon juice, if you like. If not serving immediately, pour extra olive oil over the top of the sauce, cover and leave to one side until required.

Stir the sauce well and add a little more lemon juice or salt and pepper, if you like. Spoon 1 tablespoon of sauce over each fillet. Serve with lemon wedges, sautéed potatoes, if you like, and with the remaining sauce.

COOK'S TIP
Any leftover Chimichurri Sauce can be stored up to 1 day, just pour extra olive oil over the top, cover and chill. It will lose its fresh color but the flavor will intensify.

MEDITERRANEAN WHITE FISH STEW

PREPARATION TIME: 20 minutes, plus making the stock (optional) and aïoli
COOKING TIME: 1 hour on HIGH, plus 12 minutes on LOW   **SERVES 4**

2 tablespoons olive oil

1 onion, sliced

1 leek, halved lengthwise, sliced and rinsed

4 garlic cloves, finely chopped

4 tablespoons aniseed-flavored spirit or dry white wine

3 cups Fish Stock (see page 168), weak Vegetable Stock (see page 169) or store-bought stock

4 bay leaves

2 teaspoons dry dill

1 long strip orange peel, pith removed

1 pound 5 ounces boneless, skinless mixed fish, such as hake, John Dory, monkfish, mullet, sea bream and whiting, cut into bite-size pieces

12 ounces raw shelled jumbo shrimp, deveined

1 recipe quantity Aïoli (see page 169)

salt and freshly ground black pepper

chopped parsley leaves, to serve

slices of French bread, toasted, to serve

Heat the oil in a saucepan over high heat. Lower the heat to medium, add the onion and leek and fry, stirring, 2 minutes. Add the garlic and fry 1 to 3 minutes longer until the onion is soft.

Add the alcohol and boil for a few minutes until it almost evaporates. Stir in the stock, bay leaves, dill and orange peel and season with salt and pepper. Pour the mixture into the slow cooker.

Cover the cooker with the lid and cook on HIGH 1 hour until the flavors blend. Switch the cooker to LOW, add the fish, then re-cover and cook until the fish is cooked through and flakes easily. Allow 12 minutes for pieces of fish 1 inch thick and 6 minutes for thin pieces of fish. Six minutes before the end of the cooking time, add the shrimp and cook until they turn pink and curl. Use a slotted spoon to remove and discard any bones and the bay leaves. Transfer the fish and shrimp to a bowl, cover with foil and keep warm.

Stir 2 tablespoons of the cooking liquid into the aïoli. Slowly whisk the aïoli into the cooking liquid, whisking continuously to prevent the sauce curdling. Add a little more salt and pepper, if you like. Return the fish and shrimp to the cooker and heat through, if necessary. Sprinkle with parsley and serve with toast.

THAI FISH & COCONUT CURRY

PREPARATION TIME: 20 minutes, plus making the stock (optional)
COOKING TIME: 1 hour on HIGH, plus 12 minutes on LOW **SERVES 4**

1 tablespoon sunflower oil

2 shallots, thinly sliced

2 garlic cloves, crushed

1 Thai red chili, seeded if you like, and thinly sliced

1 tablespoon shrimp paste

1 teaspoon turmeric

⅔ cup weak Vegetable Stock (see page 169) or store-bought stock

1¾ cups coconut milk

4 kaffir lime leaves

1-inch piece galangal, peeled and sliced

2 teaspoons palm sugar or soft light brown sugar, plus extra to taste

juice of 1 lime, plus extra to taste

1 teaspoon fish sauce, or to taste (optional)

1½ pounds mixed boneless, skinless white fish, such as cod, hake, halibut or pollack, cut into large chunks

freshly ground black pepper

chopped cilantro leaves, to serve

grated lime zest and lime halves, to serve

cooked basmati rice, to serve

bottled or canned red chilies in vinegar, drained and sliced (optional), to serve

Heat the covered slow cooker on HIGH. Heat the oil in a large skillet over high heat. Lower the heat to medium, add the shallots and fry 2 minutes. Add the garlic and chili and fry 1 to 3 minutes longer until the shallots are soft. Stir in the shrimp paste, then sprinkle the turmeric over.

Add the stock, coconut milk, lime leaves, galangal, palm sugar and lime juice and season with pepper. Bring to a boil, stirring to dissolve the shrimp paste and sugar, then pour the mixture into the cooker.

Cover the cooker with the lid and cook on HIGH 1 hour until the flavors blend. Add the fish sauce, if using, and add a little more sugar and lime juice, if you like.

Switch the cooker to LOW. Add the fish, re-cover and cook until the fish is cooked through and flakes easily. Allow 12 minutes for pieces of fish 1 inch thick and 6 minutes for thin pieces of fish.

Remove and discard the galangal. Sprinkle with cilantro and lime zest and serve with lime halves, rice and sliced red chilies, if you like.

FISHERMAN'S SUPPER

Cooking squid either has to be lightning fast, or slow and gentle, making squid an ideal candidate for cooking in a slow cooker. With chorizo, saffron and a hint of chili, this recipe is inspired by numerous seafood stews along the Iberian coast.

PREPARATION TIME: 20 minutes, plus making the croutes (optional)
COOKING TIME: 8 hours 20 minutes on LOW   **SERVES 4**

2 tablespoons olive oil

5 ounces fresh chorizo, skinned and sliced

1 fennel bulb, thinly sliced with the fronds reserved

4 garlic cloves, crushed

a large pinch saffron threads

a pinch red pepper flakes (optional)

½ cup dry white wine

2 cans (15-oz.) crushed tomatoes

12 new potatoes, scrubbed and halved or quartered if large, or 1 can (15-oz.) chickpeas, drained and rinsed

7 ounces fresh or thawed, frozen squid rings

1½ pounds mixed fish, such as cod, hake, halibut, mullet or porgy, on the bones and cut into large chunks

salt and freshly ground black pepper

1 recipe quantity Anchovy Croutes (see page 171), to serve (optional)

Heat 1 tablespoon of the oil in a large skillet over high heat. Lower the heat to medium, add the chorizo and fry, stirring, 1 to 2 minutes until it gives off its fat and starts to crisp. Use a slotted spoon to transfer the chorizo to the slow cooker.

Heat the remaining oil in the pan. Add the fennel and fry, stirring, 2 minutes. Add the garlic and fry 1 to 3 minutes longer until the fennel is soft. Stir in the saffron and red pepper flakes, if using.

Add the wine and boil until it almost evaporates. Add the crushed tomatoes and potatoes and season with salt and pepper. Bring to a boil, stirring, and boil 3 minutes. Pour the mixture into the cooker and stir in the squid rings.

Cover the cooker with the lid and cook on LOW 8 hours until the squid rings and potatoes are tender. Use a large metal spoon to skim any excess fat from the surface of the cooking liquid, then stir.

Add the fish, re-cover and cook until the fish is cooked through and flakes easily. Allow 20 minutes for thick pieces of fish on the bone, 12 minutes for boneless fish 1 inch thick and 6 minutes for thin pieces. Add a little more salt and pepper, if you like. Sprinkle with the reserved fennel fronds and serve with Anchovy Croutes, if you like.

MOCK PAELLA

PREPARATION TIME: 15 minutes, plus making the stock (optional) and at least 5 minutes standing
COOKING TIME: 1 hour 15 minutes on HIGH   **SERVES 4**

1 tablespoon olive oil

1 large onion, finely chopped

4 garlic cloves, finely chopped

9 ounces fresh chorizo, skinned and diced

½ teaspoon smoked paprika

3 cups Chicken Stock (see page 168), Vegetable Stock (see page 169) or store-bought stock, plus extra if needed

1 pound 2 ounces fresh or thawed, frozen mixed shellfish, such as mussels, shrimp and squid rings

1½ cups easy-cook white rice

2 red bell peppers, halved lengthwise, seeded and diced

a large pinch saffron threads

½ teaspoon salt, or to taste

⅓ cup frozen peas, thawed

4 tablespoons chopped parsley leaves

freshly ground black pepper

Heat the oil in a saucepan over high heat. Lower the heat to medium, add the onion and fry, stirring, 2 minutes. Add the garlic and fry 1 to 3 minutes longer until the onion is soft. Add the chorizo and paprika and stir 1 minute, then use a metal spoon to remove any excess oil.

Add the stock, increase the heat to high and bring to a boil, then pour the mixture into the slow cooker. Stir in the shellfish, rice, peppers, saffron and salt, then season with pepper.

Cover the cooker with the lid and cook on HIGH 1 hour. Stir in the peas, re-cover and cook 15 minutes longer until the rice is tender and the peas are cooked through. Add a little more salt and pepper, if you like.

Switch the cooker off. Put a clean dish towel over the paella, re-cover with the lid and leave to stand at least 5 minutes. The paella can be left covered with the dish towel up to 30 minutes. Just before serving, stir in the parsley. Serve hot.

SHRIMP & CRAB GUMBO

PREPARATION TIME: 50 minutes, plus making the stock (optional)
COOKING TIME: 1 hour 40 minutes on HIGH   **SERVES 4**

1 pound 2 ounces large unshelled shrimp, shelled, heads removed and deveined, with heads and shells reserved

½ cup Fish Stock (see page 168) or store-bought stock

3 tablespoons corn oil

3 ounces andouille sausage or fresh chorizo, skinned and sliced

½ cup all-purpose flour

1 large onion, chopped

4 garlic cloves, chopped

1 celery stick, halved lengthwise and chopped

1 red bell pepper, halved lengthwise, seeded and diced

1 green bell pepper, halved lengthwise, seeded and diced

1 can (15-oz.) crushed tomatoes

1 cup chopped green beans

4 okra, trimmed and sliced

2 bay leaves, torn

1 tablespoon sweet paprika

1 tablespoon dry dill

2 teaspoons dry thyme

½ teaspoon red pepper flakes (optional)

½ pound fresh white crabmeat, picked over

salt and freshly ground black pepper

finely chopped scallions, to serve

cooked long-grain rice, to serve (optional)

hot pepper sauce, to serve

Put the reserved shrimp shells and heads and the stock in a small saucepan and simmer, covered, over medium-low heat until required.

Meanwhile, heat the oil in a skillet over high heat. Lower the heat to low, add the sausage and fry, stirring, 10 minutes until it gives off its fat. Use a slotted spoon to transfer the sausage to the slow cooker.

Sprinkle the flour into the remaining oil in the pan and stir to make a thick paste. Continue stirring 15 to 20 minutes until the paste turns a hazelnut color. It will be very slow to change color, then change quickly, so watch closely so it does not burn.

Add the onion, garlic, celery and peppers and stir 3 to 5 minutes longer until the onion is soft. Add the crushed tomatoes, green beans, okra, bay leaves, paprika, dill, thyme and red pepper flakes, if using.

Strain the stock into the pan, discarding the solids, and bring to a boil, stirring. Season with salt and pepper, then pour the mixture into the cooker.

Cover the cooker with the lid and cook on HIGH 1½ hours until the mixture is thick. Stir in the shrimp and crabmeat, re-cover the cooker and cook 10 minutes longer until the shrimp turn pink and curl. Remove and discard the bay leaves and add a little more salt and pepper, if you like. Sprinkle with scallions, and serve with rice, if you like, and with hot pepper sauce for adding at the table.

VEGETARIAN

The recipes in this chapter highlight the exciting tastes of cuisines with a strong vegetarian culture. I particularly like vegetarian food from the Mediterranean and Far East—hearty casseroles and slowly simmered curries that are ideal for preparing in the slow cooker.

The Vegetable Tagine (see page 141) captures the spicy flavors of North Africa, while the Chickpea Curry (see page 138) and Lentil Dahl (see page 142) are inspired by Indian cooking. The Thai-inspired Vegetable & Cashew Red Curry (see page 145) is a fragrant, warming recipe served with naan bread to make a satisfying meal. Claypot-Style Chinese Vegetables & Tofu (see page 146) is subtle and soothing at the end of a long day. It has become quite a favorite in my house.

Risottos are also one of my favorite foods but they are not naturally suited to being made in slow cookers. Pumpkin & Dolcelatte Rice (see page 132) has many similar characteristics, however, and the melting cheese added at the end of cooking provides the desired creaminess.

I hope this chapter provides inspiration for non-vegetarians, too. The recipes are packed with flavor and are very satisfying!

◄ RATATOUILLE (SEE PAGE 135)

PUMPKIN & DOLCELATTE RICE

This is as close as I think you can get to making an authentic risotto in a slow cooker. It has all the flavor of an Italian classic.

PREPARATION TIME: 20 minutes, plus making the stock (optional)
COOKING TIME: 1½ hours on LOW **SERVES 4**

1 tablespoon olive oil, plus extra for greasing

1 cup halved lengthwise, thinly sliced and rinsed leeks

2 large garlic cloves, chopped

½ cup arborio rice

1 teaspoon dry sage

4 tablespoons dry white vermouth or dry white wine

2 cups Vegetable Stock (see page 169) or store-bought stock, plus extra if needed

¼ teaspoon salt, plus extra to taste

3 cups peeled, seeded and chopped pumpkin

heaped ½ cup rinded and coarsely chopped dolcelatte cheese

freshly ground black pepper

2 tablespoons pumpkin seeds, toasted (see page 170), to serve

snipped chives, to serve

Grease the inside of the slow cooker container. Heat the oil in a large skillet over high heat. Reduce the heat to medium, add the leeks and fry, stirring, 2 minutes. Add the garlic and fry 1 to 3 minutes longer until the leeks are soft. Stir in the rice and sage.

Add the vermouth and boil until it evaporates. Add the stock and salt and season with pepper, then bring to a boil. Pour the mixture into the cooker and stir in the pumpkin.

Cover the cooker with the lid and cook on LOW 1½ hours until the rice and pumpkin are tender.

When the rice and pumpkin are tender, add the dolcelatte and gently stir until it melts into the rice. Add a little more salt and pepper, if you like. Sprinkle with the toasted pumpkin seeds and chives and serve.

RATATOUILLE

Serve this ever-popular vegetable stew straight from the cooker, or leave it to cool completely and enjoy with a selection of salads.

PREPARATION TIME: 20 minutes, plus making the stock (optional)
COOKING TIME: 4½ hours on HIGH   **SERVES 4**

5 tablespoons olive oil or garlic-flavored olive oil, plus extra to serve

2 cups peeled and chopped eggplant

2 tablespoons herbes de Provence or Italian mixed herbs

1 large onion, chopped

4 large garlic cloves, chopped

1 zucchini, halved lengthwise and thickly sliced

1 red bell pepper, halved lengthwise, seeded and sliced

1 can (15-oz.) plum tomatoes

½ cup tomato puree

2 tablespoons Vegetable Stock (see page 169) or store-bought stock

1 teaspoon soft brown sugar

salt and freshly ground black pepper

basil leaves, to serve

French bread, to serve (optional)

Heat 2 tablespoons of the oil in a large skillet over high heat. Reduce the heat to medium, add half of the eggplant and fry, stirring, 5 to 8 minutes until it absorbs the oil and begins to soften, then use a slotted spoon to transfer it to the slow cooker. Add another 2 tablespoons oil and repeat with the remaining eggplant. Sprinkle the herbs into the cooker.

Heat the remaining oil in the pan. Add the onion and fry, stirring, 2 minutes. Add the garlic and fry 1 to 3 minutes until the onion is soft.

Transfer the onion and garlic to the cooker. Add the zucchini, pepper and plum tomatoes. Pour the tomato puree and stock over, stir in the brown sugar and season with salt and pepper. The vegetables will not be completely covered with liquid.

Cover the cooker with the lid and cook on HIGH 4½ hours, stirring once after 2 hours, until the vegetables are tender. Add a little more salt and pepper, if you like. Sprinkle with basil and serve hot or at room temperature with French bread drizzled with oil, if you like.

STUFFED PEPPERS

PREPARATION TIME: 20 minutes, plus making
  the stock (optional)
COOKING TIME: 5 hours on LOW   **SERVES 4**

2 tablespoons garlic-flavored olive oil
1 red onion, finely chopped
3 tablespoons pine nuts, coarsely chopped
1 garlic clove, finely chopped
½ cup easy-cook white or brown rice
1 cup Vegetable stock (see page 169) or store-bought
  stock, boiling
⅓ cup currants or raisins
2 tablespoons tomato paste
2 tablespoons chopped parsley leaves
2 tablespoons chopped mint leaves
½ teaspoon ground cinnamon
4 large red bell peppers that will fit upright in the
  slow cooker, tops cut off and reserved and seeded
1 cup bottled tomato sauce, boiling
1 small handful of basil leaves, chopped
salt and freshly ground black pepper

Heat 1 tablespoon of the oil in a skillet over medium
heat. Add the red onion and fry, stirring, 2 minutes.
Add the pine nuts and garlic and fry 1 to 3 minutes
longer until the pine nuts are golden.

Transfer the mixture to a large bowl. Add the
rice, stock, currants, tomato paste, parsley, mint,
cinnamon and the remaining oil. Season with salt
and pepper. Divide the mixture into the peppers,
including all the liquid. Stand the peppers upright
in the cooker, using foil to support them, if necessary,
then top with the lids. Pour the tomato sauce into
the container and push the basil into the sauce.

Cover the cooker with the lid and cook on LOW
5 hours until the rice is tender. Serve hot or chilled.

TABBOULEH TOMATOES

PREPARATION TIME: 20 minutes, plus making
  the stock and halloumi (optional)
COOKING TIME: 1½ hours on LOW   **SERVES 4**

4 large tomatoes, about 9 ounces each, that will fit
  upright in the slow cooker
2 garlic cloves, peeled
¾ cup Vegetable Stock (see page 169)
  or store-bought stock, boiling
8 sun-dry tomatoes in oil, drained and finely chopped
⅔ cup coarse bulgur wheat
4 tablespoons chopped mint leaves, plus extra
  to serve
4 tablespoons chopped parsley leaves
½ teaspoon ground allspice
a pinch cayenne pepper, or to taste (optional)
salt and freshly ground black pepper
2 tablespoons pine nuts, toasted (see page 170),
  to serve
1 recipe quantity Fried Halloumi (see page 172),
  to serve (optional)

Cut the top off each tomato and reserve. Scoop out
the pulp and seeds and discard. Sprinkle the insides
with salt, then turn upside-down to drain.

Put the garlic on a cutting board, sprinkle with salt
and use a knife to crush to a paste. Put the garlic
paste, stock, sun-dry tomatoes, bulgur wheat, mint,
parsley, allspice and cayenne pepper, if using,
in a bowl and stir. Season with salt and pepper.

Divide the mixture into the tomatoes, then top with
the lids. Stand the tomatoes upright in the slow
cooker, using foil to support them, if necessary.

Cover the cooker with the lid and cook on LOW
1½ hours until the bulgur wheat is tender. Sprinkle
with toasted pine nuts and mint and serve hot or
cold with Fried Halloumi, if you like.

CHICKPEA CURRY

PREPARATION TIME: 15 minutes, plus making
 the stock (optional)
COOKING TIME: 4 hours on LOW, plus 15 minutes
 on HIGH   **SERVES 4**

2 cans (15-oz.) chickpeas, drained and rinsed
4 large garlic cloves, finely chopped
1½-inch piece gingerroot, peeled and chopped
1 tablespoon ghee, peanut oil or sunflower oil
2 teaspoons cumin seeds
1 large onion, finely chopped
2 tablespoons Madras curry powder
a pinch red pepper flakes, to taste (optional)
1 can (15-oz.) crushed tomatoes
¼ cup Vegetable Stock (see page 169)
 or store-bought stock
4 tablespoons tomato puree
7 ounces baby spinach leaves, rinsed and shaken dry
salt and freshly ground black pepper
garam masala, to serve
warm naan breads, to serve

Put the chickpeas in the slow cooker. Put the garlic
and ginger in a mini food processor and process
until a coarse paste forms, then leave to one side.

Melt the ghee in a skillet over high heat. Reduce
the heat, add the cumin seeds and stir 30 seconds.
Add the onion and fry 3 to 5 minutes. Add the garlic
paste, curry powder and red pepper flakes, if using,
and fry 30 seconds. Add the crushed tomatoes, stock
and tomato puree and bring to a boil, stirring, then
season. Pour the mixture into the cooker.

Cover the cooker with the lid and cook on LOW
4 hours. Switch the cooker to HIGH and stir in the
spinach. Cook, uncovered, 10 to 15 minutes, stirring
once, until tender. Sprinkle with garam masala and
serve with naan breads.

TWO-BEAN CHILI

PREPARATION TIME: 20 minutes, plus 8 hours
 soaking the beans
COOKING TIME: 2 hours on HIGH, plus 8 hours
 on LOW   **SERVES 4**

1¼ cups dry kidney beans, soaked in cold water
 at least 8 hours
¼ cup dry cannellini beans, soaked in cold water
 at least 8 hours
4 garlic cloves, chopped
1 celery stick, chopped
1 onion, chopped
2 tablespoons ancho chili powder or cayenne pepper
1 tablespoon dry thyme
1 tablespoon dry mint
2 teaspoons ground coriander
2 teaspoons ground cumin
2 cans (15-oz.) crushed tomatoes
salt and freshly ground black pepper
chopped cilantro leaves, to serve
sour cream, to serve

Bring a large, covered saucepan of unsalted
water to a boil. Drain all of the beans and
add them to the pan. Return to a boil and boil
vigorously 10 minutes. Drain and rinse the beans,
then transfer them to the slow cooker.

Add all of the remaining ingredients, then pour
1 cup boiling water over and stir, adding a little
extra water to cover the beans, if necessary. Season
with pepper.

Cover the cooker with the lid and cook on HIGH
1 hour. Switch the cooker to LOW and cook 10 hours
until the beans are tender. Season with salt and
a little more pepper, if you like. Sprinkle with cilantro
and serve with sour cream.

BEANS & LENTILS WITH KALE

PREPARATION TIME: 25 minutes, plus at least 8 hours soaking the legumes, and
making the stock and croutes (optional)
COOKING TIME: 6 hours 20 minutes on HIGH   **SERVES 4**

¼ cup dry mung beans, soaked in cold water at least 8 hours

¼ cup dry white beans, such as cannellini, soaked in cold water at least 8 hours

2 tablespoons split black lentils, soaked in cold water at least 8 hours

2 tablespoons green lentils, soaked in cold water at least 8 hours

2 tablespoons split red lentils, soaked in cold water at least 8 hours

heaped 1 cup diced potatoes, such as Yukon Gold

8 garlic cloves, peeled

1 celery stick, thinly sliced

1 onion, grated

1 tablespoon celery seeds

1 tablespoon dry marjoram or dry oregano

2 cups Vegetable Stock (see page 169) or store-bought stock, boiling, plus extra if needed

1 cup tomato puree

2 teaspoons soft light brown sugar

1 cup chopped green beans

2 cups rinsed and sliced kale

salt and freshly ground black pepper

chopped parsley leaves, to serve

1 recipe quantity Cheese & Mustard Croutes (see page 171), to serve (optional)

Bring a large, covered saucepan of unsalted water to a boil. Drain all of the beans and lentils and add them to the pan. Re-cover the pan, return to a boil and boil vigorously 10 minutes.

Meanwhile, put the potatoes, garlic, celery, onion, celery seeds and marjoram in the slow cooker.

At the end of the boiling time, drain and rinse the beans, then transfer to the cooker. Pour the stock over, adding extra to cover the beans and lentils, if necessary, and season with pepper.

Cover the cooker with the lid and cook on HIGH 6 hours until all the beans and lentils are tender.

Add the tomato puree, brown sugar, green beans and kale. Cook, uncovered, 20 minutes longer until the green beans and kale are tender. Season with salt and a little more pepper, if you like. Sprinkle with parsley and serve with Cheese & Mustard Croutes, if you like.

VEGETABLE TAGINE

PREPARATION TIME: 25 minutes, plus making the stock (optional)
COOKING TIME: 5 hours on LOW, plus 20 minutes on HIGH   **SERVES 4**

1 can (15-oz.) chickpeas, drained and rinsed

1 cup diced sweet potato

1 cup peeled and diced eggplant

¾ cup diced carrot

2 tablespoons olive oil

1 large onion, finely chopped

4 garlic cloves, finely chopped

2 red bell peppers, halved lengthwise, seeded and chopped

2 tablespoons harissa paste

½ teaspoon red pepper flakes (optional)

1 can (15-oz.) crushed tomatoes

1 cup Vegetable Stock (see page 169) or store-bought stock

½ cup tomato puree

½ cup black olives, pitted

4 sun-dry tomatoes in oil, drained and finely chopped

1 preserved lemon, sliced

2 tablespoons dry parsley

2 tablespoons dry basil

½ teaspoon sugar

1 cup diced zucchini

⅔ cup golden raisins or raisins

salt and freshly ground black pepper

cilantro or mint sprigs, to serve

cooked couscous, to serve

Put the chickpeas, sweet potato, eggplant and carrot in the slow cooker.

Heat the oil in a large skillet over high heat. Lower the heat to medium, add the onion and fry, stirring, 2 minutes. Add the garlic and peppers and fry 1 to 3 minutes longer until the onion is soft. Add the harissa paste and red pepper flakes, if using, and stir 30 seconds longer.

Add the crushed tomatoes, stock, tomato puree, olives, sun-dry tomatoes, preserved lemon, parsley, basil and sugar and season with salt and pepper. Bring to a boil, stirring, then pour the mixture into the cooker and stir together. The vegetables will not be completely covered with liquid.

Cover the cooker with the lid and cook on LOW 5 hours until the vegetables are tender.

Add the zucchini and golden raisins. Switch the cooker to HIGH and cook, uncovered, 20 minutes until the zucchini is tender. Remove and discard the preserved lemon slices and add a little more salt and pepper, if you like. Sprinkle with cilantro and serve with couscous.

(4)

LENTIL DAHL

PREPARATION TIME: 15 minutes
COOKING TIME: 4 hours on HIGH   **SERVES 4**

⅔ cup split chana dal or dry yellow split peas, rinsed

⅓ cup split red lentils, rinsed

1 onion, grated

1½-inch piece gingerroot

4 large garlic cloves, chopped

½ teaspoon turmeric

a large pinch ground asafetida

salt and freshly ground black pepper

garam masala, to serve

cilantro leaves, to serve

warm naan breads, to serve (optional)

TEMPERING

4 tablespoons ghee, or 2 tablespoons peanut oil or sunflower oil with 2 tablespoons butter

2 dry red chilies, halved

2 teaspoons cumin seeds

1 teaspoon black mustard seeds

2 large tomatoes, seeded and diced

Put the chana dal, lentils and onion in the slow cooker and pour 3½ cups boiling water over.

Peel and coarsely chop half the ginger. Put the chopped ginger and garlic in a mini food processor and process until a coarse paste forms, scraping down the side of the bowl as necessary. Add the paste to the cooker with the turmeric and asafetida and season with pepper.

Cover the cooker with the lid and cook on HIGH 4 hours until the lentils are tender. Grate the remaining unpeeled ginger directly into the pot and season with salt and a little more pepper, if you like. Use a wooden spoon to stir and mash some of the lentils against the side of the container.

When the lentils are tender, make the tempering. Melt the ghee in a skillet over high heat. Add the chilies, cumin seeds and mustard seeds and stir about 30 seconds until the seeds crackle. Add the tomatoes and continue stirring 1 to 2 minutes longer until they are soft. Watch closely so the seeds do not burn.

Ladle the dahl into bowls, then top with the tempering spices. Sprinkle with garam masala and cilantro and serve with naan breads, if you like.

(5)

VEGETABLE & CASHEW RED CURRY

PREPARATION TIME: 20 minutes
COOKING TIME: 5 hours on LOW   **SERVES 4**

1½ cups peeled, seeded and diced butternut squash

1½ cups cauliflower cut into small flowerets

3 tablespoons peanut oil or sunflower oil, plus extra if needed

1 red onion, finely chopped

4 garlic cloves, finely chopped

1½ cups eggplant cut into chunks

3 tablespoons Thai red curry paste

1½ cups coconut milk

4 ounces snow peas, trimmed

⅔ cup unsalted cashew nuts

2 kaffir lime leaves

juice of ½ lime, plus extra to taste

salt and freshly ground black pepper

1 red chili, seeded and thinly sliced, to serve

cilantro leaves, to serve (optional)

2 tablespoons pumpkin seeds, toasted (see page 170), to serve (optional)

naan breads, warm, to serve

Put the squash and cauliflower in the slow cooker.

Heat 1 tablespoon of the oil in a large skillet over high heat. Reduce the heat to medium, add the red onion and fry, stirring, 2 minutes. Add the garlic and fry 1 to 3 minutes longer until the onion is soft. Use a slotted spoon to transfer the onion and garlic to the cooker.

Heat the remaining oil in the pan. Add the eggplant and fry, stirring, until soft. Add a little extra oil, if necessary. Stir in the curry paste and stir 1 minute.

Add the coconut milk and bring to a boil, stirring, then pour the mixture into the cooker. Stir in the snow peas, cashew nuts, lime leaves and lime juice and season with salt and pepper.

Cover the cooker with the lid and cook on LOW 5 hours until the squash and cauliflower are tender.

When the vegetables are tender, stir well and add a little more lime juice, salt and pepper, if you like. Sprinkle with red chili and with cilantro and toasted pumpkin seeds, if you like. Serve with warm naan breads.

CLAYPOT-STYLE CHINESE VEGETABLES & TOFU

PREPARATION TIME: 25 minutes, plus making the stock (optional)
COOKING TIME: 1½ hours on LOW, plus 20 minutes on HIGH **SERVES 4**

1½ cups broccoli cut into small flowerets

1 cup cauliflower cut into small flowerets

3 ounces baby corn cobs, halved lengthwise

3 ounces snow peas

1 carrot, thinly sliced

12 dry shiitake mushrooms, rinsed well

1 tablespoon peanut oil

1 onion, finely chopped

4 garlic cloves, chopped

1 tablespoon Chinese five-spice powder

2 cups Vegetable Stock (see page 169) or store-bought stock

2 tablespoons soy sauce, plus extra to taste

1 tablespoon soft light brown sugar

4 cloves

1 cinnamon stick

1 star anise

a pinch ground Szechuan pepper, plus extra to taste (optional)

2 cups cored and finely shredded Chinese cabbage

1 cup fried tofu, drained and cut into bite-size pieces

freshly ground black pepper

toasted sesame oil, to serve

2 scallions, finely shredded, to serve

Put the broccoli, cauliflower, baby corn cobs, snow peas, carrot and shiitake mushrooms in the slow cooker.

Heat the oil in a skillet over high heat. Reduce the heat to medium, add the onion and fry, stirring, 2 minutes. Add the garlic and fry 1 to 3 minutes longer until the onion is soft. Add the Chinese five-spice powder and stir 30 seconds.

Add the stock, soy sauce, brown sugar, cloves, cinnamon stick, star anise and Szechuan pepper, if using, and season with black pepper. Bring to a boil, stirring to dissolve the sugar, then pour the mixture into the cooker. The vegetables will not be completely covered with liquid.

Cover the cooker with the lid and cook on LOW 1½ hours until the mushrooms are tender and the vegetables are tender but still retain a slight bite. Add the Chinese cabbage and add a little more soy sauce, Szechuan pepper and black pepper, if you like.

Switch the cooker to HIGH, re-cover and cook 10 minutes. Add the tofu and cook 10 minutes longer until the cabbage is tender. Discard the cloves, cinnamon stick and star anise.

Use a slotted spoon to divide the mushrooms, vegetables and tofu into bowls, then ladle the broth over. Drizzle with toasted sesame oil, sprinkle with scallions and serve.

BUCKWHEAT, MUSHROOM & PEA CASSEROLE

PREPARATION TIME: 15 minutes, plus making the stock (optional) and 10 minutes standing
COOKING TIME: 1½ hours on LOW, plus 15 minutes on HIGH   **SERVES 4**

1 tablespoon garlic-flavored olive oil

2 onions, finely chopped

4 garlic cloves, finely chopped

1 tablespoon dry rosemary

6 cups sliced cremini mushrooms

½ ounce dry porcini mushrooms

½ cup buckwheat groats

¾ cup Vegetable Stock (see page 169) or store-bought stock, plus extra if needed

4 tablespoons tomato paste

1 teaspoon hot paprika, or to taste

a pinch sugar

1 cup frozen peas, thawed

2 tablespoons chopped parsley leaves

2 tablespoons snipped chives

salt and freshly ground black pepper

sunflower seeds, to serve

sour cream, to serve (optional)

Heat the oil in a large skillet over high heat. Lower the heat to medium, add the onions and fry, stirring, 2 minutes. Add the garlic and rosemary and fry 1 to 3 minutes longer until the onions are soft. Add the cremini mushrooms, sprinkle with salt and continue to fry until all the liquid is absorbed.

Put the porcini mushrooms in a sieve and rinse under cold running water to remove any dirt. Add the buckwheat, stock, tomato paste, paprika, sugar and the rinsed porcini mushrooms and stir until the tomato paste dissolves, then season with pepper. Transfer the ingredients to the slow cooker.

Cover the cooker with the lid and cook on LOW 1½ hours until the buckwheat is tender. Stir in the peas, parsley and chives and add a little more salt and pepper, if you like. Switch the cooker to HIGH, re-cover and cook 15 minutes until the peas are tender.

Switch off the cooker. Put a clean dish towel over the container, re-cover with the lid and leave to stand 10 minutes for the steam to be absorbed. Just before serving, fluff up the buckwheat with a fork, then sprinkle with sunflower seeds and serve with sour cream, if you like.

DESSERTS

Don't overlook using your slow cooker when it comes to making desserts.
The slow, gentle cooking technique makes slow cookers ideal for replacing
a bain-marie in the oven, or a steamer on the stovetop, and for poaching fruit.
Anybody who enjoys making desserts will enjoy the flexibility
of using a slow cooker.

Egg-based desserts are conventionally cooked in a bain-marie to prevent the eggs
curdling. You can create the same effect in your slow cooker, producing an Almond
Crème Caramel (see page 159) or Pots de Crème au Chocolat (see page 157) with
satin-smooth textures. The slow cooker's low cooking temperature also make
it ideal for desserts that are traditionally steamed on the hob, such as
Spiced Bread Pudding (see page 165).

Date Pudding (see page 163) and Lemon Pudding (see page 164) are both great recipes
for rounding off winter meals, but during warmer times of the year, try Summer Fruit
with Polenta & Almond Topping (see page 156). I also enjoy the Winter Fruit Salad
(see page 154) with a dollop of Greek yogurt for a breakfast on the run.

One word of caution with the recipes in this chapter: select a bowl or dish that fits
in your slow cooker with the lid in place before you start cooking. You can improvise
with whatever you have in your cupboard, as long as the volume capacity remains the
same as specified in the recipe.

◄ WINTER FRUIT SALAD (SEE PAGE 154)

SPICED FIGS

PREPARATION TIME: 15 minutes
COOKING TIME: 1¼ hours on HIGH
SERVES 4

⅔ cup apple juice
½ cup soft light brown sugar
1 tablespoon honey
1 cinnamon stick
a pinch ground cloves
1 vanilla bean, split lengthwise, or ½ teaspoon
   vanilla extract
24 dry figs
1 teaspoon lemon juice (optional)
vanilla ice cream, crème fraîche or sour crream,
   to serve

Put the apple juice, brown sugar and honey
in the slow cooker. Stir until the sugar and honey
dissolve, then add the cinnamon stick, cloves and
vanilla bean.

Cover the cooker with the lid and cook on HIGH
45 minutes. Add the figs, re-cover and cook
30 minutes longer until they are soft but holding
their shape. Serve the figs hot with scoops
of ice cream.

Alternatively, serve the figs with a thicker syrup.
Use a slotted spoon to transfer the figs to a bowl,
then leave to one side. Pour the syrup and spices
into a small saucepan and boil over high heat
8 minutes, or until it reduces. If the syrup is too
sweet, stir in the lemon juice. Pour it over the figs
and serve with scoops of ice cream.

If not serving immediately, leave the figs to cool
completely, then cover and chill until required. The
figs can be kept in the refrigerator up to 1 week.

CHERRY & KIRSCH COMPOTE

PREPARATION TIME: 20 minutes, plus cooling
COOKING TIME: 1½ hours on HIGH   **SERVES 4**

1 cup sugar
1 vanilla bean, split lengthwise, or ½ teaspoon
   vanilla extract
2 pounds cherries, stems removed
2 tablespoons blanched almonds
1 tablespoon kirsch
2 tablespoons slivered almonds, toasted (see page
   170), to decorate
vanilla or chocolate ice cream, to serve (optional)

Heat the covered slow cooker on HIGH while you
assemble the ingredients.

Put the sugar in the cooker and pour ½ cup boiling
water over. Stir until the sugar dissolves, then add
the vanilla bean.

Cover the cooker with the lid and cook on HIGH
45 minutes. Add the cherries and blanched
almonds, then re-cover the cooker and cook
45 minutes longer until the cherries are tender.

Strain into a bowl, reserving the syrup, and leave
the cherries and syrup to cool separately. When the
cherries are cool, remove the vanilla bean and the
blanched almonds. When the syrup is cool, stir
in the cherries and kirsch.

Sprinkle with slivered almonds and serve with
scoops of ice cream, if you like. If not serving
immediately, cover and chill until required.
The compote can be kept in the refrigerator
up to 3 days.

VANILLA & PEPPER-POACHED PEARS

PREPARATION TIME: 15 minutes, plus cooling, at least 2 hours chilling, and making the sauce (optional)
COOKING TIME: 1 hour 50 minutes on HIGH **SERVES 4**

1½ cups sweet white wine or orange juice

½ cup sugar

1 vanilla bean, split lengthwise

1 tablespoon black peppercorns, lightly crushed

thinly pared peel of 1 large orange, pith removed, plus extra finely grated orange zest, to decorate

4 pears, such as Conference, about 7 ounces each

1 recipe quantity Hot Chocolate Sauce (see page 175), to serve (optional)

Heat the covered slow cooker on HIGH while you assemble the ingredients.

Put the wine, sugar, vanilla bean, peppercorns and orange peel in the cooker, and stir until the sugar dissolves.

Cover the cooker with the lid and cook on HIGH 1½ hours.

Fifteen minutes before the end of the cooking time, peel the pears, leaving the stems intact. Use an apple corer or small metal spoon to remove the cores from the bottom of each pear, then level the bottom with a knife so the pears stand upright.

Put the pears in the cooker and spoon the wine mixture over them. The pears will only be half submerged in the liquid. Re-cover the cooker and cook 20 minutes longer until the pears are tender but holding their shape. Use a slotted spoon to remove the pears from the cooker, then transfer them to a bowl and leave to cool completely.

Transfer the cooking juices to a small saucepan and boil until they reduce by two-thirds. Strain the syrup into a bowl and discard the orange peel and peppercorns. Leave the syrup to cool completely.

Once cooled, spoon the syrup over the pears. Cover and chill at least 2 hours and up to 48 hours. Sprinkle the pears and syrup with orange zest and serve with Hot Chocolate Sauce, if you like.

COOK'S TIP
The vanilla beans can be wiped, dried and used again.

WINTER FRUIT SALAD

It's best to use firm dry fruit for this, rather than the plumped "ready-to-eat" varieties. If, however, you only have the softer fruit in your cupboard, reduce the cooking time in the second step to 1 hour before you add the smaller fruit.

PREPARATION TIME: 10 to 15 minutes, plus 30 minutes steeping
COOKING TIME: 2½ hours on HIGH   **SERVES 4**

1 pound dry fruit, such as apples, apricots, mangoes or prunes

1 cup orange juice, plus extra if needed

8 green cardamom pods, lightly crushed

6 Earl Grey tea bags

1 cinnamon stick

thinly pared peel of 1 lemon, pith removed

thinly pared peel of 1 orange, pith removed

⅓ cup soft light brown sugar, plus extra if needed

2 tablespoons dry cranberries

2 tablespoons currants

2 tablespoons golden raisins

2 tablespoons hazelnuts (optional)

lemon juice, to taste (optional)

Greek yogurt or plain yogurt, to serve

Put the dry fruit, orange juice, cardamom pods, tea bags, cinnamon stick and lemon and orange peels in the slow cooker—do not turn the cooker on. Pour 3 cups boiling water over, then cover with the lid and leave to steep 30 minutes.

Switch the cooker to HIGH. Remove and discard the tea bags. Add the brown sugar and stir until it dissolves. Re-cover the cooker and cook 1½ hours. Stir in the cranberries, currants and golden raisins, re-cover and cook 1 hour longer until all the fruit is soft and the flavors blend.

Meanwhile, toast the hazelnuts, if using. Heat a skillet over medium heat, add the hazelnuts and dry-fry 3 to 4 minutes until light brown, shaking the pan occasionally so they do not burn. Leave to cool slightly, then rub off the skins, chop and leave to one side.

When the fruit salad is cooked, taste and add lemon juice, if you like, or a little more orange juice or brown sugar, depending on how tart the fruit is. Sprinkle with the toasted hazelnuts, if using, and serve hot with dollops of yogurt. If not serving immediately, leave the salad to cool completely, then cover and chill until required. Leftovers can be kept refrigerated in an airtight container up to 1 week.

SUMMER FRUIT WITH POLENTA & ALMOND TOPPING

PREPARATION TIME: 20 minutes, plus 5 minutes standing
COOKING TIME: 4½ hours on HIGH　　**SERVES 4**

3 cups mixed summer berries, such as blackberries and raspberries

3 baking apples, such as Granny Smiths, peeled, cored and chopped

2 tablespoons soft light brown sugar, plus extra if needed

2 teaspoons arrowroot or cornstarch

finely grated zest of 1 orange

confectioners' sugar, to decorate

vanilla ice cream, to serve (optional)

POLENTA & ALMOND TOPPING

5 tablespoons butter, soft

⅓ cup sugar

1 extra-large egg plus 1 extra-large yolk, beaten together

¾ teaspoon almond extract

½ cup medium polenta or yellow cornmeal

½ cup self-rising flour

¾ teaspoon baking powder

2 tablespoons slivered almonds

Select a 6-inch soufflé dish or 3-cup heatproof dish that will fit in the slow cooker with the lid in place and leave to one side. Line the bottom of the container with foil, then heat the covered cooker on HIGH.

Put the berries and apples in a saucepan. Sprinkle the brown sugar and arrowroot over and toss lightly to coat the fruit. Put the pan over high heat and stir gently until the sugar dissolves and the juices start to run. Stir in the orange zest and add a little more sugar, if you like, depending on how tart the fruit is. Turn off the heat, cover and leave to stand while you make the topping.

To make the topping, put the butter and sugar in a large bowl and beat until light and fluffy. Beat in the eggs and almond extract, then beat in the polenta. Sift the flour and baking powder over and fold in, using a metal spoon.

Return the fruit to high heat and bring to a boil. Pour the fruit and juices into the dish, then immediately spoon the topping in 4 to 6 mounds over the top—the topping will be too stiff to spread but it will meld together as it cooks. Sprinkle the almonds over the top and put the dish in the cooker.

Cover the cooker with the lid and cook on HIGH 4½ hours until the topping is set.

Remove the dish and leave to stand 5 minutes. Sift some confectioners' sugar over and serve with scoops of ice cream, if you like.

①

POTS DE CRÈME AU CHOCOLAT

PREPARATION TIME: 15 minutes, plus cooling and at least 4 hours chilling
COOKING TIME: 1 hour on LOW   **SERVES 4**

5 extra-large egg yolks

2 cups heavy cream, plus ¼ cup to serve

2 tablespoons sugar, plus 4 tablespoons to serve

¼ teaspoon vanilla extract

a pinch salt

4 ounces dark chocolate, 70% cocoa solids, chopped, plus ½ ounce to serve

Select four ⅔-cup heatproof pots that will fit in the slow cooker with the lid in place and leave to one side.

Beat the egg yolks in a large heatproof bowl. Put the cream, sugar, vanilla extract and salt in a small saucepan over medium heat and stir until the sugar dissolves. Increase the heat to high and bring to a boil. Add the chocolate and stir until it melts.

Add the chocolate mixture to the egg yolks, whisking constantly, until blended. Strain the mixture into a large measuring jug, then pour into the pots. Cover the top of each pot with plastic wrap, then put them in the cooker. Pour enough boiling water into the container to reach halfway up the sides of the pots.

Cover the cooker with the lid and cook on LOW 1 hour until the custards are set around the edge but slightly wobbly in the middles. Carefully lift the chocolate pots out of the cooker, then remove the plastic wrap and leave to cool completely. Re-cover with fresh plastic wrap and chill at least 4 hours and up to 24 hours. The custards will firm up as they chill.

Just before serving, whip the ¼ cup cream until soft peaks form. Sprinkle the 4 tablespoons sugar over and whip until stiff. Add a spoonful of cream to the top of each pot, then grate the dark chocolate over and serve.

ALMOND CRÈME CARAMEL

PREPARATION TIME: 15 minutes, plus cooling and at least 12 hours chilling
COOKING TIME: 1½ hours on LOW   **SERVES 4**

heaped ½ cup sugar, plus 1 tablespoon extra

a drop of lemon juice

2½ cups milk

4 eggs

¼ teaspoon almond extract

2 tablespoons slivered almonds, toasted (see page 170), to serve

Put an upturned, heatproof saucer in the slow cooker.

Put the sugar and ½ cup water in a small stainless-steel saucepan over medium heat and stir until the sugar dissolves. Increase the heat to high and boil 3 to 5 minutes without stirring, until the caramel turns a dark golden brown color. Watch closely because it can burn quickly. Immediately remove the pan from the heat and add the lemon juice to stop the cooking process. Pour the caramel into a 6-inch soufflé dish and leave to one side.

Put the milk in a clean saucepan and heat over high heat until it just reaches boiling point, then remove the pan from the heat. Put the eggs, almond extract and extra sugar in a bowl and beat until the sugar dissolves. Add the milk and mix together, beating constantly. Strain the egg mixture over the caramel, and cover the top with plastic wrap. Put the dish on top of the saucer in the slow cooker. Pour enough boiling water into the container to reach halfway up the side of the dish.

Cover the cooker with the lid and cook on LOW 1½ hours until the custard is set and a knife inserted in the middle comes out clean. Remove the crème caramel from the cooker, uncover and leave to cool completely, then cover and chill at least 12 hours.

Just before serving, run a knife around the edge of the dish. Place a rimmed serving dish upside-down over the top of the soufflé dish, hold the two firmly together, invert and shake. Carefully remove the soufflé dish. Sprinkle with almonds and serve. This is best made at least 1 day before serving; it will keep in the refrigerator up to 3 days.

CREAMY RICE PUDDING

PREPARATION TIME: 10 minutes
COOKING TIME: 1½ hours on HIGH   **SERVES 4**

butter, soft, for greasing

3 tablespoons sugar

2 tablespoons cornstarch

2¾ cups milk

½ cup pudding rice or other short-grain rice

a pinch salt

finely grated zest of 1 lemon, plus extra to decorate

2 teaspoons lemon juice, or to taste (optional)

2 tablespoons chopped pistachio nuts, to serve

freshly grated nutmeg, to serve

½ cup heavy cream, to serve, if needed

Grease the bottom and sides of the slow cooker container. Heat the covered cooker on HIGH while you assemble the ingredients.

Put the sugar and cornstarch in the cooker. Slowly whisk in the milk, and continue whisking until the sugar and cornstarch dissolve—make sure there are not any lumps. Stir in the rice and salt.

Cover the cooker with the lid and cook on HIGH 15 minutes. Stir well, making sure to incorporate any cornstarch that has sunk to the bottom of the container. Re-cover the cooker and cook 15 minutes longer, then stir again.

Stir in the lemon zest, re-cover and cook 1 hour longer, without stirring, until the rice is tender and the pudding is thick and creamy. Slowly stir in a little lemon juice, if using. Sprinkle with extra lemon zest, pistachios and nutmeg and serve hot.

If not serving immediately, transfer to the rice pudding to a bowl and leave to cool completely, then cover and chill up to 24 hours. The pudding will thicken quite a bit, so stir in the cream, if necessary, and serve chilled with extra lemon zest, pistachio and nutmeg.

DATE PUDDING

PREPARATION TIME: 20 minutes, plus making the sauce
COOKING TIME: 1½ hours on HIGH   **SERVES 4**

½ cup pitted dates, chopped

½ teaspoon baking soda

5 tablespoons butter, soft, plus extra for greasing

½ cup sugar

1 egg, beaten

½ teaspoon vanilla extract

1 cup self-rising flour

a pinch salt

1 recipe quantity Dark Toffee Sauce (see page 175), to serve

vanilla ice cream, to serve (optional)

Put an upturned heatproof saucer in the slow cooker. Grease a 6-inch soufflé dish or a 3-cup heatproof dish that will fit on top of the saucer with the cooker lid in place. Cut out a circle of foil to cover the top of the dish with a 1-inch overhang and leave to one side.

Put the dates, baking soda and 1 cup water in a saucepan over medium heat and simmer, stirring occasionally, 5 minutes, until the dates are soft. Remove the pan from the heat and leave to cool slightly.

Put the butter and sugar in a large bowl and beat until light and fluffy, then beat in the egg and the vanilla extract. Sift the flour and salt into the bowl and beat it in. Add the dates and their soaking liquid and fold in.

Spoon the batter into the prepared dish and smooth the surface. Cover the dish with plastic wrap, then with the foil, and tie a piece of string tightly around the rim of the dish to secure it. Put the dish on top of the saucer, then pour enough boiling water into the container to reach halfway up the side of the dish.

Cover the cooker with the lid. Cook on HIGH 1½ hours until the pudding is firm to the touch and a skewer inserted in the middle comes out clean.

Remove the date pudding from the cooker. Carefully remove the foil and plastic wrap and leave to stand in the dish 2 minutes. Serve with hot Dark Toffee Sauce and scoops of ice cream, if you like.

8

LEMON PUDDING

PREPARATION TIME: 20 minutes, plus 5 minutes standing, and making the sauce (optional)
COOKING TIME: 8 hours on HIGH   **SERVES 4**

½ cup butter, soft, plus extra for greasing

½ cup sugar

2 eggs

½ teaspoon vanilla extract

1½ cups self-rising flour

a pinch salt

3 tablespoons finely grated lemon zest, or a mixture of lemon, lime and orange zests

3 to 4 tablespoons lemon juice

1 recipe quantity Butterscotch Sauce (see page 175), to serve (optional)

Put an upturned heatproof saucer in the slow cooker. Grease a 4-cup pudding bowl or heatproof bowl that will fit on top of the saucer with the cooker lid in place. Line the bottom of the bowl with parchment paper, then grease the paper. Cut out a circle of foil to cover the top of the bowl with a 1-inch overhang and set aside.

Put the butter and sugar in a large bowl and beat until light and fluffy, then beat in the eggs, one at a time, and the vanilla extract. Sift the flour and salt over, add the lemon zest and fold in. Gradually stir in the lemon juice until the mixture is a soft dropping consistency.

Spoon the mixture into the prepared bowl and smooth the surface. Cover the bowl with plastic wrap, then with the foil, and tie a piece of string tightly around the rim of the bowl to secure it. Put the bowl on top of the saucer, then pour enough boiling water into the container to reach halfway up the side of the bowl.

Cover the cooker with the lid and cook on HIGH 8 hours until the pudding is well risen and a skewer inserted in the middle comes out clean. Remove the lemon pudding from the cooker. Carefully remove the foil and plastic wrap and leave the pudding to stand in the bowl 5 minutes.

Run a knife around the edge of the bowl. Place a rimmed serving dish upside-down over the bowl, hold the two firmly together, invert, giving a firm shake halfway over. Remove the bowl, peel off the parchment paper and serve with hot Butterscotch Sauce, if you like.

SPICED BREAD PUDDING

PREPARATION TIME: 15 minutes, plus 22 minutes standing, and making the sauce (optional)
COOKING TIME: 5 hours on HIGH   **SERVES 4**

4 tablespoons butter, plus extra for greasing

¾ cup milk

2 teaspoons apple pie spice

finely grated zest of 1 orange

a pinch salt

10 ounces day-old white bread, torn into small pieces

scant 1 cup soft light brown sugar, plus 2 tablespoons extra

1¼ cups mixed ready-to-eat dry fruit, such as apricots, cranberries, currants, raisins and golden raisins, chopped, if necessary

½ teaspoon almond extract

2 eggs, beaten

1 recipe quantity Fresh Orange Sauce (see page 175), to serve (optional)

Grease a 6- x 4½-inch bread pan or 3-cup heatproof dish that will fit in the slow cooker with the lid in place and leave to one side. Heat the covered cooker on HIGH, while you assemble the ingredients.

Put the butter, ½ cup of the milk, spice, orange zest and salt in a large saucepan over medium heat and bring to a simmer. Add the bread, brown sugar, dry fruit and almond extract, and stir until the bread is soft. Remove the pan from the heat and leave to stand 20 minutes.

Beat in the eggs, then add enough of the remaining milk to form a soft and moist, but not mushy, mixture. Spoon the mixture into the prepared pan and sprinkle the extra brown sugar over the top. Cover the pan with plastic wrap and put it in the cooker.

Cover the cooker with the lid and cook on HIGH 5 hours until the pudding is set.

Remove the bread pudding from the cooker and leave to stand in the pan 2 minutes. Remove the plastic wrap and run a knife around the edges of the pan. Place a cutting board over the pudding, hold the two firmly together, invert, giving a firm shake halfway over, and remove the pan. Slice the pudding and serve with hot Fresh Orange Sauce, if you like.

COOK'S TIP
Any leftover bread pudding can be eaten at room temperature, making it ideal for including in lunchboxes.

TRADITIONAL PLUM PUDDING

A slow cooker really comes into its own at Christmas. Use it to make or reheat the pudding, freeing stovetop space. To reheat, cover with plastic wrap and foil as below, add to the cooker on an upturned saucer and pour enough boiling water into the container to come halfway up the side of the bowl. Cover and reheat on HIGH 3 hours.

PREPARATION TIME: 25 minutes, plus 45 minutes standing and making the sauce
COOKING TIME: 6 hours on HIGH   **SERVES 4**

1¼ cups raisins

¾ cup currants

½ cup golden raisins

6 tablespoons brandy or orange juice

1 cooking apple, peeled, cored and grated

2 extra-large eggs, beaten

¾ cup grated suet

2 cups fresh bread crumbs

½ cup self-rising flour

⅓ cup very finely ground blanched almonds

⅓ cup firmly packed soft dark brown sugar

2 tablespoons chopped candied lemon peel

2 tablespoons chopped candied orange peel

1 tablespoon apple pie spice

1 teaspoon ground cloves

½ teaspoon ground nutmeg

a pinch salt

butter, for greasing

1 recipe quantity Hard Sauce (see page 175), to serve

Put the raisins, currants, golden raisins and brandy in a bowl. Leave to stand 30 minutes. Add all the remaining ingredients and stir.

Meanwhile, put an upturned heatproof saucer in the slow cooker. Grease a 4-cup pudding bowl or heatproof bowl that will fit on top of the saucer with the cooker lid in place. Line the bottom of the bowl with parchment paper, then grease the paper. Cut out a circle of foil to cover the top of the bowl with a 1-inch overhang and set aside.

Spoon the plum pudding mixture into the bowl and smooth the surface. The mixture will be about 1-inch below the rim. Cover the bowl with plastic wrap, then with the foil and tie a piece of string tightly around the rim of the bowl to secure it. Put the bowl on top of the saucer, then pour enough boiling water into the container to reach halfway up the side of the bowl.

Cover the cooker with the lid and cook on HIGH 6 hours until set. Remove the pudding from the cooker. Carefully remove the foil and plastic wrap and leave to stand in the bowl 15 minutes. Place a serving plate upside-down over the pudding, hold the two firmly together, invert, giving a firm shake halfway over, and remove the bowl. Peel off the parchment paper. Serve hot with Hard Sauce.

BASIC RECIPES & ACCOMPANIMENTS

STOCKS

BEEF STOCK

Don't be tempted to skip the first step. It is this slow browning that gives the stock its dark brown color and depth of flavor.

PREPARATION TIME: 50 minutes
COOKING TIME: 10 hours on LOW
MAKES ABOUT 4½ cups

1 pound beef bones, chopped
1 pound boneless beef shin, trimmed and
   cut into large chunks
1 carrot, sliced
1 celery stick, sliced
1 onion, sliced
2 bay leaves, tied together with several parsley sprigs and
   thyme sprigs
1 teaspoon black peppercorns

Heat the oven to 425°F. Put the beef bones, beef shin, carrot, celery and onion in a roasting pan and roast 40 minutes, stirring often.

Transfer the beef, bones and vegetables to the slow cooker. Add the herb bundle and peppercorns and pour 5 cups water over.

Cover the cooker and cook on LOW 10 hours. Use a large metal spoon to skim any excess fat from the surface of the cooking liquid, then strain the stock into a large bowl, discarding the solids.

If not using immediately, leave to cool completely, then cover and chill. Once chilled, remove any fat from the surface. Keep refrigerated and use within 2 days or freeze up to 3 months.

CHICKEN STOCK

If I'm not in the mood or don't have time to make stock after I've roasted a chicken, I simply put the bones in the freezer until I want them. If you do this, be sure to thaw the bones and let them come to room temperature before adding them to the slow cooker.

PREPARATION TIME: 10 minutes
COOKING TIME: 10 hours on LOW
MAKES ABOUT 5½ cups

1 large carrot, sliced
1 celery stick, chopped
1 onion, sliced
2 teaspoons black peppercorns, lightly crushed
2 tablespoons Italian mixed herbs or dried parsley
1½ pounds cooked chicken carcass or bones, chopped
   to fit in the slow cooker
salt

Put the carrot, celery, onion, peppercorns, mixed herbs and chicken in the slow cooker and pour 6 cups water over.

Cover the cooker and cook on LOW 10 hours. Strain the stock into a large bowl, discarding the solids.

If not using immediately, leave to cool completely, then cover and chill. Once chilled, remove any fat from the surface. Keep refrigerated and use within 2 days or freeze up to 3 months.

FISH STOCK

PREPARATION TIME: 10 minutes
COOKING TIME: 2 hours on LOW
MAKES ABOUT 6 cups

1 onion, sliced
1 bay leaf, tied together with several parsley sprigs and
   a piece leek
1 teaspoon black peppercorns, lightly crushed
1½ pounds white fish heads, bones and trimmings

Put the onion, herb bundle and peppercorns in the slow cooker, then top with the fish heads, bones and trimmings. Pour 6½ cups water over.

Cover the cooker and cook on LOW 45 minutes. Use a large metal spoon to skim any foam from the surface of the cooking liquid. Re-cover the cooker and cook 1¼ hours longer. Strain the stock into a large bowl, discarding the solids.

If not using immediately, leave to cool completely, then cover and chill. Keep refrigerated and use within 1 day or freeze up to 3 months.

....

VEGETABLE STOCK

PREPARATION TIME: 10 minutes
COOKING TIME: 8 hours on LOW
MAKES ABOUT 5½ cups

4 celery sticks, chopped, with the tops reserved
1 carrot, sliced
1 leek, sliced and rinsed
1 onion, sliced, with the skin reserved, if you like
2 bay leaves, tied together with several parsley sprigs and thyme sprigs
1 teaspoon black peppercorns, lightly crushed

Put the celery, carrot, leek, onion, herb bundle, peppercorns and the onion skin, if using, in the slow cooker—the onion skin gives stock a dark golden color. Pour 6 cups water over, adding extra to cover all of the vegetables, if necessary.

Cover the cooker and cook on LOW 8 hours. Strain the stock into a large bowl, discarding the solids.

If not using immediately, leave to cool completely, then cover and chill. Keep refrigerated and use within 2 days or freeze up to 3 months.

OTHER BASIC RECIPES

....

AÏOLI

PREPARATION TIME: 15 minutes
MAKES enough for 1 fish stew

2 egg yolks
8 garlic cloves, roughly chopped
1¼ cups extra virgin olive oil

1 teaspoon lemon juice, plus extra to taste
salt and freshly ground black pepper

Put the egg yolks and garlic in a mini food processor and process until the garlic is pureed. With the motor running, slowly add the olive oil, drop by drop, and continue to process until incorporated. As the sauce begins to thicken add the oil in a steady stream until thickened and smooth.

Add 1 teaspoon warm water and the lemon juice and season with salt and pepper. Blend again and add a little more lemon juice and salt and pepper, if you like.

If not using immediately, transfer the aïoli to a bowl and cover. Keep refrigerated up to 1 day before using.

....

CHEESE & HERB DUMPLINGS

PREPARATION TIME: 10 minutes
SERVES 4

¾ cup dried bread crumbs
heaped ½ cup self-rising flour
4 tablespoons cold butter, diced
½ cup coarsely grated strong cheese, such as cheddar or Parmesan
1 tablespoon finely snipped chives
1 tablespoon finely chopped parsley leaves

Put the bread crumbs, flour and butter in a blender or food processor and blend until the mixture resembles coarse crumbs. Transfer to a bowl, then add the cheese and herbs and combine the ingredients. Wet your hands, divide the mixture into 8 equal portions and roll into balls.

If not using immediately, cover and keep refrigerated up to 6 hours before cooking.

....

GREMOLATA

PREPARATION TIME: 10 minutes
SERVES 4

1 garlic clove, finely chopped
peel of 1 lemon, pith removed and finely chopped
2 tablespoons finely chopped parsley leaves

Put all the ingredients in a small bowl and mix until combined.

JALFREZI CURRY PASTE

PREPARATION TIME: 10 minutes
MAKES enough for 1 recipe quantity of curry

2 garlic cloves, chopped
1½-inch piece gingerroot, peeled and chopped
2 tablespoons tomato paste
1 tablespoon ground coriander
1 tablespoon ground cumin
2 teaspoons tamarind paste
a pinch cayenne pepper, or to taste

Put the garlic and ginger in a mini food processor and process until a coarse paste forms. Add all the remaining ingredients and process again, scraping down the side of the bowl as necessary, until blended.

If not using immediately, refrigerate in an airtight container up to 1 week, or freeze up to 1 month.

MASSAMAN CURRY PASTE

PREPARATION TIME: 10 minutes
MAKES enough for 1 recipe quantity of curry

1 tablespoon tamarind paste
4-inch piece lemongrass stem, tough outer leaves
   discarded and finely chopped
½-inch piece gingerroot, peeled and finely chopped
2 large garlic cloves, chopped
1 dried red chili, seeded if you like, and chopped
1 Thai or small shallot, chopped
2 teaspoons shrimp paste
1½ teaspoons ground coriander
1½ teaspoons ground cumin
1½ teaspoons fish sauce
½ teaspoon ground cardamom
½ teaspoon ground cinnamon
¼ teaspoon grated nutmeg
a pinch ground cloves

Put all the ingredients in a mini food processor and process 1 to 2 minutes until a thick paste forms, scraping down the side of the bowl as necessary, until well combined.

If not using immediately, refrigerate in an airtight container up to 1 week, or freeze up to 1 month.

FINISHING TOUCHES

TOASTED SEEDS & NUTS

COOKING TIME: 1 to 3 minutes

sesame seeds
pumpkin seeds
pine nuts
slivered almonds

Heat a dry skillet until hot. Reduce the heat to medium, add the seeds or nuts and dry-fry 1 to 2 minutes for sesame seeds, or 2 to 3 minutes for pumpkin seeds, pine nuts and slivered almonds, until light brown. (Shake the pan occasionally so they do not burn.) Remove the pan from the heat and immediately tip the seeds or nuts out of the pan.

ACCOMPANIMENTS

TO SERVE WITH SOUPS

GARLIC CROUTONS

Don't waste the garlic cloves after they flavor the oil in your pan—they can be added to soups just before pureeing for a real garlic hit, or crush them onto toast.

PREPARATION TIME: 5 minutes
COOKING TIME: 10 minutes
SERVES 4

4 tablespoons olive oil, plus extra if needed
4 garlic cloves, peeled
4 slices day-old bread, crusts removed and cut into cubes
salt

Heat the oil in a skillet over medium-low heat. Add the garlic and fry, stirring, 3 to 5 minutes, until light brown. Use a slotted spoon to remove the garlic.

Increase the heat to medium, add the bread cubes and fry, turning occasionally, 3 to 5 minutes until golden brown and crisp, working in batches to avoid overcrowding the pan and adding extra oil, if necessary. Drain on paper towels, then sprinkle with salt.

If not using immediately, leave to cool completely, then store in an airtight container up to 5 days.

MAPLE CREAM

PREPARATION TIME: 3 minutes
SERVES 4

6 tablespoons sour cream
1 tablespoon maple syrup, plus extra to taste
a pinch freshly grated nutmeg, plus extra to taste

Put the sour cream in a small bowl and beat until smooth. Beat in the maple syrup and nutmeg, adding extra to taste, if you like.

If not using immediately, cover and keep refrigerated up to 4 hours before serving.

PESTO SAUCE

This is best made just before serving, however, if you do make it in advance, cover the surface with a thin layer of olive oil to preserve the fresh green color.

PREPARATION TIME: 10 minutes
SERVES 4

2 ounces basil leaves
3 tablespoons freshly grated Parmesan cheese
   or pecorino cheese
2 garlic cloves, coarsely chopped
1 tablespoon pine nuts
½ cup extra virgin olive oil, plus extra
   if needed
salt and freshly ground black pepper

Put the basil in a mini food processor, sprinkle with salt and process until finely chopped. Add the Parmesan, garlic and pine nuts and process again until finely chopped.

Transfer to a bowl, stir in the olive oil and season with salt and pepper.

If not using immediately, drizzle a thin layer of olive oil over, cover and set aside up to 4 hours before serving.

TO SERVE WITH MAIN COURSES

ANCHOVY CROUTES

PREPARATION TIME: 5 minutes
COOKING TIME: 6 minutes
SERVES 4

1 can (2-oz.) anchovies in oil
1 garlic clove, finely chopped
2 tablespoons finely chopped parsley leaves
¼ teaspoon smoked or sweet paprika
4 large slices country bread

Put the anchovies and their oil in a small saucepan over high heat and stir until the anchovies dissolve into the oil. Stir in the garlic, parsley and paprika, then remove from the heat and set aside.

Meanwhile, heat the broiler to high and position the broiler rack 2 inches from the heat source. Toast the bread 2 to 3 minutes on each side until golden brown and crisp.

Spread the anchovy mixture over each slice of toast, then cut each slice into 3 "fingers." Serve hot.

CHEESE & MUSTARD CROUTES

PREPARATION TIME: 5 minutes
COOKING TIME: 7 minutes
SERVES 4

4 slices sourdough or other bread
4 tablespoons wholegrain or Dijon mustard, or to taste
1 cup finely grated Gruyère or cheddar cheese
sweet or smoked paprika
vegetarian Worcestershire sauce

Heat the broiler to high and position the broiler rack 2 inches from the heat source. Toast the bread 2 to 3 minutes on each side until golden brown and crisp.

Spread the mustard over each slice of toast, then divide the cheese onto the slices. Sprinkle paprika and a few drops of Worcestershire sauce over the top of each slice. Return to the broiler and broil about 1 minute until the cheese melts and starts to bubble, then cut each slice into 3 "fingers." Serve hot.

CUCUMBER & MINT RAITA

PREPARATION TIME: 5 minutes, plus 20 minutes standing
SERVES 4

1 cucumber, seeded and sliced
4 tablespoons thinly sliced mint leaves
1 cup plain yogurt
salt and freshly ground black pepper

Put the cucumber in a colander, sprinkle with salt and leave to stand in the sink 20 minutes.

Rinse the cucumber well and pat dry with paper towels. Transfer it to a bowl, add the mint and yogurt and mix well, then season with pepper.

If not serving immediately, cover and keep refrigerated up to 4 hours. Just before serving, season with salt and stir.

CUCUMBER & TOMATO RAITA

PREPARATION TIME: 5 minutes, plus 20 minutes standing
SERVES 4

1 cucumber, seeded and diced
1 red onion, finely chopped
1 large tomato, seeded and finely chopped
1¼ cups plain yogurt
salt and freshly ground black pepper
ground coriander, to serve
ground paprika or cayenne pepper, to serve
finely shredded cilantro leaves, to serve

Put the cucumber in a colander, sprinkle with salt and leave to stand in the sink 20 minutes.

Rinse the cucumber well and pat dry with paper towels. Transfer it to a bowl, then add the red onion, tomato and yogurt and mix well. Season with pepper.

If not serving immediately, cover and keep refrigerated up to 4 hours. Just before serving, season with salt and stir, then dust with ground coriander and paprika and sprinkle with cilantro leaves.

EGG & PARSLEY SAUCE

PREPARATION TIME: 10 minutes, plus 30 minutes infusing
COOKING TIME: 20 minutes
SERVES 4

1¾ cups milk
½ onion, chopped
3 cloves
1 bay leaf
1½ teaspoons thyme leaves
a pinch freshly grated nutmeg, or to taste
2 extra-large eggs, at room temperature
3 tablespoons butter
¼ cup all-purpose flour
⅓ cup crème fraîche or sour cream
2 teaspoons anchovy essence
6 tablespoons finely chopped parsley leaves
salt and freshly ground black pepper

Put the milk, onion, cloves, bay leaf, thyme and nutmeg in a saucepan and season with pepper. Bring to a boil over high heat. Remove the pan from the heat, cover and leave to infuse at least 30 minutes.

Put the eggs in a saucepan. Fill the pan with enough boiling water to cover the eggs by about 1 inch. Bring to a boil over high heat, then turn the heat down to low and simmer 10 minutes. Drain the eggs and set aside until cool enough to handle, then shell and finely chop.

Gently reheat the infused milk and bring to a simmer. Melt the butter in a clean saucepan over low heat, then add the flour and stir until smooth. Remove the pan from the heat and slowly strain the milk mixture into the flour mixture, a little at a time, stirring until a smooth sauce forms. Discard the solids.

Return the pan to the heat and bring to a boil, then reduce the heat to very low and simmer 2 minutes.

Stir the eggs into the sauce with the crème fraîche, anchovy essence and parsley. Season with salt and a little more pepper, if you like. Serve hot.

FRIED HALLOUMI

PREPARATION TIME: 5 minutes
COOKING TIME: 5 minutes
SERVES 4

8 ounces halloumi, drained and thinly sliced
extra virgin olive oil, for frying, plus extra to serve
freshly ground black pepper

Heat a large, heavy-bottomed skillet over high heat. Brush the pan with a very thin layer of olive oil and heat until it shimmers.

Reduce the heat to medium-low, add the halloumi and fry 1 to 2 minutes until golden brown, working in batches, if necessary. Use a metal spatula to gently turn the cheese over and fry on the other side until golden. Season with pepper. Serve hot, drizzled with extra olive oil.

HORSERADISH & DILL CREAM

PREPARATION TIME: 5 minutes
SERVES 4

⅔ cup sour cream
1 tablespoon freshly grated horseradish, or to taste
1 tablespoon finely chopped dill sprigs
salt

Put the sour cream, horseradish and dill in a small bowl, season with salt and mix well.

If not using immediately, cover and keep refrigerated up to 10 hours before serving.

PICKLED BEAN SPROUTS

When you first mix the ingredients together, the brine is very salty but it mellows after about half an hour. Don't make these more than two hours in advance or they lose their crispness.

PREPARATION TIME: 5 minutes, plus cooling and at least 30 minutes chilling
SERVES 4

½ cup rice vinegar
2 teaspoons salt
½ teaspoon grated palm sugar or white sugar
2 cups bean sprouts, rinsed
1 long, thin red chili, seeded and very thinly sliced
1 tablespoon very finely snipped chives
   or shredded scallions

Put the vinegar, salt and sugar in a small saucepan over medium heat and stir until the sugar dissolves. Remove the pan from the heat and leave to cool completely.

Transfer the brine to a nonmetallic serving bowl and stir in the bean sprouts and chili, making sure the bean sprouts are coated in the brine.

Cover and chill at least 30 minutes before serving, but not any longer than 2 hours. Serve sprinkled with chives.

SAFFRON RISOTTO

PREPARATION TIME: 10 minutes, plus making the stock (optional)
COOKING TIME: 25 minutes
SERVES 4

6 cups Beef Stock (see page 168), Vegetable Stock
   (see page 169) or store-bought stock
a large pinch saffron threads
1 tablespoon olive oil
2 tablespoons butter
1 onion, finely chopped
1¾ cups arborio rice
1 tablespoon dry white wine
5 tablespoons freshly grated Parmesan cheese
salt and freshly ground black pepper

Put the stock and saffron in a saucepan over medium-high heat and bring to just below a boil, then reduce the heat to a simmer.

Meanwhile, heat the oil and half of the butter in a skillet over medium heat. Add the onion and fry, stirring, 3 to 5 minutes until soft. Add the rice and stir until coated. Add the wine and leave it to bubble until it evaporates.

Add the simmering stock one ladleful at a time, stirring continuously and making sure the rice has absorbed the liquid before adding more. Continue until all the liquid has been absorbed, until all the stock has been used and the rice is tender but still retains a slight bite. This will take about 20 minutes.

Remove the pan from the heat, stir in the Parmesan and the remaining butter and season with salt and pepper. Serve hot.

SALSA VERDE

The salsa verde can be made in advance and chilled until required, but it is best made just before serving so the vibrant green color doesn't dull.

PREPARATION TIME: 5 minutes
SERVES 4

8 anchovy fillets in oil, drained and chopped
2 to 4 large garlic cloves, chopped
1 tablespoon capers in brine, rinsed
1 cup extra virgin olive oil
1 large handful basil leaves
1 large handful parsley leaves

Put the anchovies, garlic, capers and 2 tablespoons of the olive oil in a mini food processor and process until chopped but not pureed.

Add the basil and parsley and process again until finely chopped, then transfer to a serving bowl and stir in the remaining olive oil.

If not using immediately, cover and keep refrigerated up to 1 day before serving.

TORTILLA CHIPS

If you don't have a deep skillet, cut each of the longest tortilla strips in half again. This is because the longer the strips are, the more they curl and they won't cook all the way through if they are not flat.

PREPARATION TIME: 15 minutes
COOKING TIME: 12 minutes
SERVES 4

sunflower oil, for frying
4 corn tortillas, 6 inches each, cut into ½-inch strips
ancho chili powder or cayenne pepper, for sprinkling
salt and freshly ground black pepper

Line a plate with paper towels and set aside. Heat a 2-inch layer of oil in a deep skillet over medium-high heat until very hot. To test if the oil is hot enough, drop a piece tortilla into the oil—it should sizzle immediately.

Working in batches, add the tortilla strips and deep-fry, stirring, 2 to 3 minutes until golden brown and crisp. Use a slotted spoon to remove the chips from the pan and drain on the paper-lined plate. Season with salt and pepper and sprinkle with chili powder. Leave to cool completely, then toss until evenly coated in the seasonings.

If not serving immediately, store in an airtight container up to 2 days.

WATERCRESS SAUCE

PREPARATION TIME: 5 minutes
COOKING TIME: 5 minues
SERVES 4

2 ounces watercress, any thick stems removed
2 tablespoons chopped chervil
2 tablespoons chopped dill
2 tablespoons finely chopped parsley leaves
¼ teaspoon lemon juice, or to taste
¾ cup crème fraîche or sour cream
salt and freshly ground black pepper

Bring a small saucepan of unsalted water to a boil. Add the watercress and blanch 30 seconds, then immediately drain and refresh under cold running water. Squeeze to remove as much water as possible.

Put the watercress, chervil, dill and parsley in a mini food processor and process until finely chopped.

Transfer to a bowl, stir in the lemon juice and crème fraîche and season with salt and pepper.

If not using immediately, cover and leave to one side up to 4 hours before serving.

TO SERVE WITH DESSERTS

HARD SAUCE

PREPARATION TIME: 5 minutes
SERVES 4

6 tablespoons butter, soft
⅓ cup caster sugar
1 tablespoon milk
1 tablespoon brandy
¾ cup confectioners' sugar, sifted

Put the butter in a bowl and beat until light and fluffy. Beat in the sugar, milk and brandy, then sift in the confectioners' sugar. Continue beating until well combined and the butter is light and fluffy.

If not using immediately, cover and keep refrigerated up to 2 days or freeze up to 2 months.

BUTTERSCOTCH SAUCE

PREPARATION TIME: 5 minutes
COOKING TIME: 5 minutes
SERVES 4

¾ cup sugar
4 tablespoons butter
½ cup heavy cream

Put the sugar and 4 tablespoons water in a stainless-steel saucepan over medium heat and stir until the sugar dissolves.

Increase the heat to high and boil, without stirring, until the caramel turns a dark golden brown color. Watch closely because it can burn quickly. Immediately remove the pan from the heat, add the butter and whisk it in, then whisk in the cream. Serve hot.

DARK TOFFEE SAUCE

PREPARATION TIME: 10 minutes
COOKING TIME: 10 minutes
SERVES 4

5 tablespoons butter, diced
¾ cup turbinado sugar
⅔ cup heavy cream
1 teaspoon vanilla extract

Melt the butter in a saucepan over medium heat. Add the sugar, cream and vanilla extract and stir until the sugar dissolves, then bring to a boil. Immediately reduce the heat to low and simmer 5 minutes until the sauce thickens. Serve hot.

FRESH ORANGE SAUCE

PREPARATION TIME: 10 minutes
COOKING TIME: 5 minutes
SERVES 4

1½ teaspoons arrowroot or cornstarch
1 tablespoon sugar
finely grated zest of 1 large orange
⅔ cup freshly squeezed orange juice
1 teaspoon butter
2 teaspoons orange-flavored liqueur (optional)

Put the arrowroot, sugar and orange zest in a heatproof bowl and stir together. Add 2 tablespoons of the orange juice and stir until smooth.

Put the remaining orange juice in a saucepan and bring to a boil over high heat, then beat it into the arrowroot mixture until smooth.

Return the mixture to the pan and return to a boil, stirring until the sauce is thick and clear. Beat in the butter, then stir in the liqueur, if using. Serve hot.

HOT CHOCOLATE SAUCE

PREPARATION TIME: 5 minutes, plus 30 minutes heating the cooker
COOKING TIME: 15 minutes on HIGH
SERVES 4

5 tablespoons butter, diced and soft
5 tablespoons finely chopped dark chocolate, 70% cocoa solids
2 tablespoons superfine sugar
⅛ teaspoon vanilla extract
a pinch salt

Heat the covered slow cooker on HIGH 30 minutes.

Put all of the ingredients in the cooker, then pour 3 tablespoons boiling water over and stir until the chocolate dissolves.

Cover the cooker and cook on HIGH 15 minutes. Serve the sauce hot, or leave on the WARM setting until required.

INDEX